FUSANG.

RECORDS OF ASIAN HISTORY

Report on Japan
to the Secret Committee of the East India Company
SIR STAMFORD RAFFLES

History of Japan
compiled from the Records of the East India Company
PETER PRATT

Early Records of British India
a History of the English Settlements in India
J. TALBOYS WHEELER

Baghdad during the Abbasid Caliphate
from contemporary Arabic and Persian sources
G. LE STRANGE

A History of the Moghuls of Central Asia
The Tarikh-i-Rashidi of Mirza Muhammad Haidar
N. ELIAS AND E. D. ROSS

Kogoshui
Gleanings from Ancient Stories
GENCHI KATO AND HIKOSHIRO HOSHINO

Fusang
Discovery of America by Chinese Buddhist Priests
CHARLES G. LELAND

Further volumes in preparation

FUSANG

OR

THE DISCOVERY OF AMERICA

BY

CHINESE BUDDHIST PRIESTS IN THE FIFTH CENTURY.

BY

CHARLES G. LELAND.

LONDON : CURZON PRESS
NEW YORK : BARNES & NOBLE BOOKS

First published London 1875
New Impression 1973

Published by

Curzon Press Ltd   ·   London and Dublin

and

Harper & Row Publishers Inc   ·   New York
Barnes & Noble Import Division

UK 7007 0023 4
US 06 492317 7

Reprinted in Great Britain
by Kingprint Ltd · Richmond · Surrey

PREFACE.

———◆———

It is now more than a century since the learned French sinologist Deguignes set forth, in a very ably-written paper in the " Mémoires de l'Académie des Inscriptions et Belles Lettres " (vol. xxviii., 1761), the fact that he had found in the works of early Chinese historians a statement that, in the fifth century of our era, certain travellers of their race had discovered a country which they called Fusang, and which, from the direction and distance as described by them, appeared to be Western America, and in all probability Mexico. When Deguignes wrote, his resources, both as regards the knowledge of the region supposed to have been discovered and the character of the travellers, were extremely limited, so that the skill with which he conducted his investigation, and the shrewdness of his conjectures, render his memoir, even to the present day, a subject of commendation among scholars. Few men have ever done so much or as well with such scanty and doubtful material.

The original document on which the Chinese his-

b

torians based their account of Fusang was the report
of a Buddhist monk or missionary named Hoei-shin
(Schin or Shên),[1] who, in the year 499 A.D., returned
from a long journey to the East.   This report was
regularly entered on the Year-Books or Annals of the
Chinese Empire, whence it passed, not only to the pages
of historians, but also to those of poets and writers
of romances, by whom it was so confused with absurd
inventions and marvellous tales, that even at the present day discredit is thrown by a certain class of critics
on the entire narrative.   In 1841 Carl Friedrich Neumann, Professor of Oriental Languages and History at
the University of Munich, published the original narrative of Hoei-shin from the Annals, adding to it comments of his own elucidating its statements, and advancing somewhat beyond Deguignes.   This little work I
translated into English, under the supervision of Professor Neumann, and with his aid.   I believe that, as
he revised and corrected the English version here given,
it may claim to be an accurate translation from the
Chinese text of the Year-Book, and that of Hoei-shin.
I have placed it first in this volume because it gives in
a much more perfect form than is to be found in the
memoir of Deguignes the original report on which the
entire investigation is based.   It of course includes
Professor Neumann's comments on the monk's brief
narrative ; and as these embrace many remarks on the

---

[1] Neumann gives the name as Hoei-schin ; Dr Bretschneider, as Hui-
shên.   When not translating Dr Neumann, I have written it *Hoei-shin.*

possibility of passing by sea from the Chinese to the American coast, I have thought it appropriate to place next in the series a letter from Colonel Barclay Kennon, who, as a prominent officer in the United States Coast Survey, passed several years in the North Pacific, during which time he surveyed and mapped, in company with two colleagues, the entire coast, both on the Asiatic and American sides. Colonel Kennon is of opinion that the voyage supposed to have been taken by the Buddhist monks is easily practicable, and might be effected even in an open boat—the vessel in which he himself passed both summer and winter, and in which he sailed more than 40,000 miles, having been simply a small pilot-boat. To this I have added, in further reference to certain remarks by Professor Neumann, a comment on the affinities between American and Asiatic languages, and other subjects mentioned in his text, *i.e.*, the Mound-Builders and the Images of Buddha. These are followed by extracts from, and remarks on, a series of articles by M. Gustave d'Eichthal, contributed to the *Revue Archæologique* in 1862–63, in which he defends Deguignes from an attack which the well-known Orientalist Julius Heinrich von Klaproth made upon the original memoir by the former. I believe that it will be admitted by all unprejudiced scholars, that in these ably-written and very temperate articles M. D'Eichthal has fully vindicated Deguignes, and has also contributed much very valuable material to the subject. I am far from claiming that it has been absolutely proved that Hoei-shin was in Mexico, or that he was preceded thither by " five beggar-monks from the Kingdom of Kipin." But it cannot be denied that, as further researches have been made, much which at first seemed obscure or improbable in his narrative has been cleared up. All that Hoei-shin declares he saw is not only probable, but is confirmed, almost to the minutest details, by what is now known of Old and New Mexico.

All that seems fabulous in his story, he, like Herodotus, relates from hearsay ; but it is remarkable that these wonders, which Professor Neumann was unwilling to cite, all appear at the present day to be simply exaggerations of facts which recent research has brought to light. Among the objects seen and described by the monk was the maguey plant, or great cactus, which he called the Fusang, after a Chinese plant slightly resembling it, and this name (Fusang) he applied to the country. His description of this plant, and of its many uses, is very striking. Other things peculiar to Mexico, but not known to China, were remarked, as, for instance, the absence of iron, and the fact that copper, gold, and silver were not prized, and were not used for money. The manner in which marriage was contracted in Fusang, according to his description, is not at all Chinese—I doubt if it be Asiatic—but it exists in more than one North American tribe, and something very like it was observed by a recent traveller in New Mexico.

I have in Chapter IX. called attention to a fact
which seems to have escaped both Neumann and Klaproth, though both were familiar with the literature on
which it is based. It is simply this, that the voyage of
Hoei-shin forms a portion of the somewhat extensive
literature of travel of Buddhist monks, the authenticity
of which has been vindicated by Stanislas Julien. Many
of these have been translated, and one of them, " The
Mission of Sung-yun," was recently published in English. Sung-yun travelled only nineteen years after
Hoei-shin, and was in all probability a contemporary
who had met him at the Chinese court, where such
travellers enjoyed the highest consideration. Sung-yun
had been sent to India, or the West, by the Empress
Dowager Tai-Hau, of the Wei dynasty, and it is not improbable that Hoei-shin had travelled to the East, in
like manner, by imperial order. It is evident that he
lived at a time when men of his stamp were in request
to go to the ends of the earth to spread the doctrines of
Buddha.

In 1869, some one who had read or heard of Neumann's work on the Buddhist discovery of America,
placed in the " Notes and Queries on China and Japan,"
published at Hong Kong, a request that those who
possessed information on the subject would send it
to that journal. The results were, however, trifling,
the principal communication thus elicited being an
article from Dr E. Bretschneider, in which the writer,
while expressing his opinion that Hoei-shin was a

" lying Buddhist priest," and a " consummate humbug," brought forth nothing of consequence to prove such
very positive assertions.   But as the paper forms a portion of the literature of the Fusang question, I have
included it in this volume.

MEMOIR

OF

PROFESSOR CARL FRIEDRICH NEUMANN.

MEMOIR.

CARL FRIEDRICH NEUMANN, the author of the subjoined memoir on the presumed early discovery of America by Buddhist monks, was of Jewish family, and born December 22, 1798, near Bamberg, Bavaria. He was intended for commerce, but having studied history at the Universities of Heidelberg and Munich, determined to devote his life to letters. Having become a Protestant, he was appointed professor in 1822 at the Gymnasium of Speier, whence he was dismissed in 1825 for Liberal opinions in politics. He subsequently lived for several years in Venice, Paris, and London, occupied with the study of Oriental languages. Having distinguished himself as a sinologist, he went in 1829 to China, where he remained nearly two years, occupied in collecting Chinese books. In Canton he obtained a valuable library of 10,000 volumes, which, after his return, were ceded to the Bavarian Government. In 1838 he received an appointment as professor of the Chinese and Armenian languages at the University of Munich, where he also read lectures on mathematics and modern history, which were very popular with the students. Having known him well, both in public and private, and pursued studies under his special guidance, I venture to speak with confidence and respect of his enormous learning, as well as his sound judgment in matters of scholarship.

Professor Neumann was the author of a number of works in Latin, French, and English, as well as German, two of which received prizes from the Academies of Copenhagen and Paris. His principal books are the following :—

Rerum Cretaricum Specimen. Göttingen, 1820.

Ueber die Staatsverfassung der Florentiner, von Leonardus Aretinus. Frankfurt, 1822.

Historische Versuche. Heidelberg, 1825.

Mémoires sur la Vie et les Ouvrages de David, philosophe Armenien du cinquième siècle de notre ére, et principalement sur ses traductions de quelques écrits à Aristote. Paris, 1829.

The History of Vartan, and of the Battle of the Armenians, containing an account of the religious wars between the Persians and Armenians. By Elisæus ; translated by C. F. Neumann. London, 1831.

The Catechism of the Shamans, or the Laws and Regulations of the Priesthood of Buddha in China. Translated from the Chinese, with notes and illustrations. London, 1831.

History of the Pirates who infested the Chinese Seas from 1807 to 1810. Translated from the Chinese original, with notes and illustrations. London, 1831.

Geschichte der Armenischen Literatur. Leipzig, 1833–36.

Geschichte der Uebersiedlung von 40,000 Armeniern. Leipzig, 1834.

Russland und die Tcherkessen. Stuttgart, 1840.

Geschichte des Englisch-Chinesischen Kriegs. Leipzig, 1846.
In this comprehensive work, one division is entitled, "Nord
Amerika und Frankreich in China," in which the present and
future relations of Western America and Eastern Asia are developed with great sagacity. A few years before his death,
Iskander (Alexander Herzen) wrote to me—"The Pacific will
yet be the Mediterranean of the future." Those who look forward
to such developments of civilisation and commerce will find
this book of Professor Neumann's very interesting.

Die Völker des Südlichen Russland in ihrer geschichtlichen
Entwicklung. Leipzig, 1847. To this work was awarded the
prize of the Royal Institute of Paris.

Die Reisen des Venetianers Marco Polo, Deutsch von August
Bürk. Nebst Zusätzen und Verbesserungen von C. F. Neumann.
Leipzig, 1845.

Beiträge zur Armenischen Literatur. Leipzig, 1849.

Geschichte des Englischen Reichs in Asien. Leipzig, 1857.

Professor Neumann was one of the directors of the
German Oriental Association, and published in the first
number of their magazine a biography of Dr Morrison,
the celebrated Protestant missionary to China.

I sincerely trust that the additions which I have made
to this work, in elucidation or in illustration of the idea
advanced, will be found to the purpose. They are the
result of much research,—I may honestly say, of far
more than appears in this volume, as the subject, from
its obscurity, yielded only the proverbial grain of wheat
to the wearisome bushel of chaff. I also hope that it
is free from either reckless hypothesis or easy credulity,
and that nothing will be understood to be advanced
as being more than probable.

CONTENTS.

——◆——

THE NARRATIVE OF HOEI-SHIN, WITH COMMENTS BY PROFESSOR CARL F. NEUMANN.

CHAPTER I.

PAGE

KNOWLEDGE OF FOREIGN COUNTRIES AMONG THE CHINESE, . . 3

CHINESE KNOWLEDGE OF LANDS AND NATIONS, ... 6

CHAPTER II.

IDENTITY OF THE TARTARS AND NORTH AMERICAN INDIANS ; OR,

THE ROAD TO AMERICA, AND THE PEOPLE IN IT, . . . 7

TUNGUSE EASTERN BARBARIANS, ... 8

KAMTSCHATKA IN THE TIME OF TANG, ... 15

CHAPTER III.

TAHAN OR ALIASKA, AND ITS DISCOVERY, ... 24

THE KINGDOM OF FUSANG, OR MEXICO, ... 25

OF WRITING AND CIVIL REGULATIONS IN FUSANG, ... 26

THE KINGDOM AND THE NOBLES OF FUSANG, ... 27

MANNERS AND CUSTOMS, ... 27

AMAZONIA, ... 29

CHAPTER IV.

	PAGE
REMARKS ON THE REPORT OF HOEI-SHIN,	31
THE OLDEST HISTORY OF MEXICO,	33
THE RUINS OF MITLA AND PALENQUE,	34
FUSANG, MAGUEY, AGAVE AMERICANA,	37
METALS AND MONEY,	38
LAWS AND CUSTOMS OF THE AZTECS,	39
DOMESTIC ANIMALS,	40

CHAPTER V.

CHINESE AND JAPANESE IN KAMTSCHATKA AND THE HAWAIIAN GROUP,	43
THE FUTURE OF EASTERN ASIA,	46

REMARKS ON THE TEXT OF PROFESSOR NEUMANN.

CHAPTER VI.

FUSANG AND PERU,	49

LETTER FROM COLONEL BARCLAY KENNON ON THE NAVIGATION OF THE NORTH PACIFIC OCEAN.

CHAPTER VII.

NAVIGATION OF THE NORTH PACIFIC,	63

CHAPTER VIII.

REMARKS ON COLONEL KENNON'S LETTER,	81

CHAPTER IX.

TRAVELS OF OTHER BUDDHIST PRIESTS (FROM THE FOURTH TO THE EIGHTH CENTURY A.D.),	87

AMERICAN ANTIQUITIES, WITH THEIR RELATIONS TO THE OLD WORLD.

CHAPTER X.

PAGE

AFFINITIES OF AMERICAN AND ASIATIC LANGUAGES, ... 99

CHAPTER XI.

THE MOUND-BUILDERS AND MEXICANS, ... 110

CHAPTER XII.

IMAGES OF BUDDHA, ... 119

THE ADVOCATES AND OPPONENTS OF THE NARRATIVE OF HOEI-SHIN.

CHAPTER XIII.

DEGUIGNES, KLAPROTH, AND D'EICHTHAL, ... 125

THE LATEST DISCUSSION OF FUSANG.

CHAPTER XIV.

T. SIMPSON AND DR E. BRETSCHNEIDER ; OR, EUROPEANS RESIDING IN
    CHINA ON FUSANG, ... 161

THE

NARRATIVE OF HOEI-SHIN,

WITH COMMENTS

BY

PROFESSOR CARL F. NEUMANN.

CHAPTER I.

" To retain laws and customs according to the traditionary manner, and to extend these laws and customs
to other lands," was the precept of the founders of the
Celestial Empire, as well as of other civilised nations.
" But this extension," they added, " is not to be
effected by the oratorical powers of single messengers,
nor through the force of armed hordes. This renova-
tion, as in every other sound organic growth which
forces itself from within, can only take place when the
Outer Barbarians, irresistibly compelled by the virtue
and majesty of the Son of Heaven, blush for their
barbarism, voluntarily obey the image of the Heavenly
Father, and become men."

It will be readily understood that a race holding
such opinions would undertake no voyage of discovery,
and attempt no conquests. Not a single instance
occurs during the entire four thousand years of the
history of Eastern Asia, of an individual who had
travelled in foreign lands for the purpose of adding to
his own information or that of others. The journey
of Lao-tse—the founder of the religion of the Taosse—

to the West appears to be a tale deliberately invented for the purpose of connecting his doctrine of the Primitive and Infinite Wisdom with that of " The Western Mountain of the Gods," or with Buddhism. The campaigns beyond those limits which Nature has assigned to the Chinese Empire, were undertaken merely through the impulse of self-preservation. Men were compelled, in Central as in Eastern Asia, in Thibet as well as on the banks of the Irawaddy, to anticipate the dangers and invasions which, at a later period, threatened the freedom of the Central Empire, and were frequently obliged to send ambassadors or spies into different Asiatic or European countries to obtain information relating to their situation and nature, as well as the condition of their inhabitants, which could guide them in their subsequent warlike or diplomatic relations with the enemies of the Empire.

This land, so blessed by Nature, attracted not only the barbarian desirous of plunder, but also the merchant, since certain productions, such as silk, tea, and true rhubarb, were found only there. The Chinese Government as well as people, influenced by the precepts of their wise men, received strangers graciously so long as they implicitly obeyed, or in any manner evinced fear and submission, and returned the presents which were offered according to Oriental custom with others of still greater value. All the discoveries and experiences, all the knowledge and information which they thus obtained in their peaceful or warlike relations with foreign

nations, were generally recorded in the last division
of the " Year-Books " of their own chronicles, forming,
in an historical point of view, an inestimable treasure.

In the first century of our reckoning, the pride and
vanity induced by the Chinese social system were partly
broken by the gradual progress of Buddhism over all
Eastern Asia. He who believed in the divine mission of
the son of the King of Kapilapura, must recognise every
man as his brother and equal by birth ; yes, must strive
—for the old Buddhistic faith has this in common with
the Christian religion—to extend the joyful mission of
salvation to all nations on earth, and, to attain this
end, must suffer, like the type of the God incarnate,
all earthly pain and persecution. So we find that a
number of Buddhist monks and preachers have at
distant times wandered to all known and unknown
parts of the world, either to obtain information with
regard to their distant co-religionists, or to preach the
doctrine of their Holy Trinity to unbelievers. The
official accounts which these missionaries rendered of
their travels, and of which we possess several entire,
considered as sources of information with regard to
different lands and nations, belong to the most in-
structive and important part of Chinese literature.
From these sources we have derived in a great degree
that information which we possess regarding North-
eastern Asia and the Western Coasts of America, during
centuries which have been hitherto veiled in the deepest
obscurity.

CHINESE KNOWLEDGE OF LANDS AND NATIONS.

Pride and vanity form the basis upon which the Chinese built their peculiar system of information regarding other lands and people. Around "the Flower of the Centre," as their sages teach, dwell rude uncivilised races, which are in reality animals, although they have externally human forms. To these rough brutes they apply all manner of abusive epithets, assigning to them the names of dogs, swine, devils, and savages, according to the four points of the compass whence they came. The occasional inquirers and writers of history among the Europeans who have thought it worth their while to cast a glance upon the as yet fallow fields of Eastern and Central Asiatic history, have blindly followed this limited system, which rests upon the narrowest geographic limits, so that races originally without connection were melted into one and the same people ; as, for instance, the numerous tribes of the Tartar family.

CHAPTER II.

THE Tunguse, Mongolians, and a great part of the
Turkish race, formed originally, according to all external organic tokens, as well as the elements of their
languages, but one people, closely allied with the
Esquimaux, the *Skräling*, or dwarf of the Norsemen,
and the races of the New World. This is the irrefut-
able result to which all the more recent inquiries
in anatomy and physiology, as well as comparative philology and history, have conduced. All the
aboriginal Americans have those distinctive tokens
which forcibly recall their neighbours dwelling on
the other side of Behring's Straits. They have the
four-cornered head, high cheek-bones, heavy jaws, large
angular eye-cavities, and a retreating forehead. The
skulls of the oldest Peruvian graves exhibit the same
tokens as the heads of the nomadic tribes of Oregon
and California. The different American languages, as
has been already proved by Albert Gallatin in his
minute researches, have such an identity, that we can,
however varied the vocabulary, at once reduce them to

one original source.[1]   In fact, all researches as to the
manner in which America was first populated lead to
one inevitable conclusion.   Since the earth has been
inhabited, these rude tribes dwelt in their separate
divisions of Asia and America.   This rough mass has,
however, during the course of centuries, been separated
by different corporeal and mental formative influences
into different nations, each with peculiar bodily distinctions, the natural consequence of higher mental influences; and various languages have been developed;
yet all of these distinctions, whether of body or of
language, of manner or custom, present internal evidence of an original unity.   This unity manifests
itself in their genealogies, the oldest historical system
of all nations by which the identity of the Turks,
Mongolians, and Tunguse is clearly proved.   Among
these Tartaric hordes we find absolutely the same
relation as that which existed among the German
nations.   The Ostrogoths and Visigoths, the West-
phalians, the northern and southern nations, belonged
originally, notwithstanding their different destinies and
culture, to the internal being of one and the same German race.

TUNGUSE EASTERN BARBARIANS.

All the numerous Tartaric hordes dwelling about
the north-east of the Central Empire were termed by

---

[1] *Vide* Memoires de la Société des Antiquaires de l'Amerique du Nord,
Partie linguistique rapport fait a l'Institut Historique, par M. Antonio
Renzi, Paris, 1842, 8vo.

the civilised natives of the South " Tonghu," " Eastern
Red Men," or savages, from which appellation we de-
rive our word Tunguse,[1] which has been subsequently
applied to an extremely limited portion of the entire
race. Among these Mongolian nations, many centuries
before Zenghis Khan (Tschinggs Chakan), the Mongolians proper were distinguished by the differently-written
name of *Wog* or *Mog*, and divided into seven hordes,
dwelling in different places, extending from the Corean
Peninsula to the distant north, over the river Amo to
the eastern sea; that is to say, to the Gulf of Anadir
or Behring's Straits. The nomadic tribes dwelling more
directly to the north they termed Peti, or Northern
Savages, and many tribes were reckoned by them as
belonging either to the Tunguse or Peti. During the
course of many centuries the Chinese acquired a sur-
prisingly accurate knowledge of the north-east coast of
Asia, extending, as their records in astronomy and
natural history prove, to the sixty-fifth degree of
latitude, and even to the Arctic Ocean.[2] Among other
accounts, they tell us of a land very far from the Central Kingdom, whose inhabitants, termed Kolihan or
Chorran, sent during the latter part of the seventh
century ambassadors to the Court at Singan. This
land lay on the North Sea; and still further to the
north, on the other side of that sea, the days were so

[1] In the " Shajrat ul Atrak," or Genealogical Tree of the Turks and
Tartars, translated by Colonel Miles, London, 1838, *Tung* or *Tungus* is
rendered " son of a Tartar."

[2] Gaubil : Observations Mathematiques, Paris, 1732, ii. 110.

long, and the nights in proportion so short, that the sun set and rose again " before one could roast a leg of mutton." [1]

The Chinese were well acquainted with the customs of these tribes, and describe them to us as resembling the Tsohuktschi or Koljuschens [2] of the present day, and other tribes of North-eastern Asia and North-western America. They had neither oxen, sheep, nor other domestic animals, but there were tribes among them which employed deer, which were there very numerous. These deer of which they speak were undoubtedly reindeer. They knew nothing of agriculture, but lived by hunting and fishing, as well as on the root of a certain plant which grew there in abundance. Their dwellings were constructed of twigs and wood, their clothes were made of furs and feathers. They laid their dead in coffins, which they placed in trees in the mountains. [3] They were ignorant of any subdivisions of the year. The Chinese were also as well acquainted with those dwelling more directly to the east, as with these inhabitants of the north.

The limits of the Chinese Empire extended, under the

[1] Mantuanlin, bk. 348, p. 6.

[2] *Koljustchi,* or *Koljuki,* signifies the peg or pin which those savages wear in the under lip, and from which the name is derived. They were subsequently termed by the Russians, who possess the land, Galloches, from the French word, merely in jest. In the course of time this name supplanted the earlier term Koljuken, so that all are now known as *Kaloschen.*

[3] This is similar to the custom of many North American Indians of the West.—C. G. L.

dynasty of Tschen, in the time of David and Solomon, to the Eastern Ocean. They knew and frequented the numerous groups of islands in the Pacific Ocean, for the sake of trade. The natives inhabiting these islands sent, on their part, messengers to the coast with presents, which are registered in the Chinese annals. It also frequently happened that China sent a portion of its discontented or superfluous population to these thinly-inhabited islands, as well as to Japan, Lieu-kuei, and Formosa, of which we have accurate historical proofs. The tribe of the Ainos, or Jebis, extending from Japan to Kamtschatka, over the Kurilean and Aleutian, or Fox Islands, to the distant north, where it touched upon the nearly-allied Esquimaux, must naturally have astonished the occasional colonists and merchants who found their way thither, by a singular distinctive bodily phenomenon, namely, an exceeding growth of hair on their bodies. Such was the case, and they were termed *Mau-schin* (or, according to the Japanese mode of pronouncing Chinese writing, *Mosin*)—*i.e.*, Hairy People, and also, from the great number of sea-crabs found in their region, *Hi-ai* (in Japanese, *Jeso*), or Crab-Barbarians.[1] And as these barbarians, like the inhabitants of the southern islands, were in the habit of tattooing figures upon their skin, they were also termed by the Chinese *Wen-schin*, or Painted People. In the course of time other names were also added, but any one acquainted with the nature

[1] Description of the Kurilean and Aleutian Islands (translated from the Russian), Ulm, 1792, p. 16.

of that part of the world and its inhabitants, readily recognises, despite the varied appellations, the same race of men in the Ainos. We are indebted to the numerous embassies which in earlier times passed between China and Japan for the greater part of the information contained in their Year-Books, relating to the north and south-easterly islands and nations. These embassies brought back with them many traditionary accounts, which were strongly tinged with fable, and yet not entirely devoid of truth. For instance, when they speak of the land of *Tschutschu,* or dwarfs, very far to the south of Japan, whose inhabitants, black and ugly and naked, kill and devour all strangers, we readily recognise the natives of Papua or New Guinea.

The Ainos were first described, under the name of Hairy People, in " The Book of Mountains and Seas," a Chinese work, written in the second or third century, and richly adorned with wonderful legends. They dwelt, according to this book, in the Eastern Sea, and were completely overgrown with hair.[1] Some of these people came, A.D. 659, in company with a Japanese embassy, to China ; they are termed in the Year-Book of Tang, " Crab-Barbarians,"[2] after which this note follows :—" They had long beards, and dwelt in the

[1] Schan-hai-king, quoted in the "Histoire des Trois Royaumes, traduite par Titsingh." Klaproth has, according to his custom, passed off the translation as his own. Paris, 1832, p. 218.

[2] Tang-schu, or, " Year-Books of Tang," bk. 220, p. 18, *v.* Mantuanlin, bk. 326, p. 23, *v.*, where the report as usual is given. Titsingh : Annales des Empereurs du Japon, Paris, 1834, p. 52. This is a remarkable coincidence in the Chinese and Japanese Year-Books.

north-east of Japan ; they laid bows, arrows, and deer-skins as presents before the throne. These were the inhabitants of Jeso, which island had, not long before, been subdued and rendered tributary by the Japanese." The report of the Japanese embassy, in their own domestic returns, is, however, much more copious and satisfactory. The queries of the Heaven's Son of Tang, and the replies of the Japanese ambassador, are there narrated as follows :—

The Ruler of Tang.—" Does the heavenly Autocrat find himself in constant tranquillity ? "

The Ambassador.—" Heaven and earth unite their gifts, and constant tranquillity ensues."

The Ruler of Tang.—" Are the Government officers well appointed ? "

The Ambassador.—" They have the grace of the Heavenly Ruler, and are well."

The Ruler of Tang.—" Is there internal peace ? "

The Ambassador.—" The Government harmonises with heaven and earth—the people have no care."

The Ruler of Tang.—" Where lies the land—this Jeso ? "

The Ambassador.—" To the north-east."

The Ruler of Tang.—" How many divisions has it ? "

The Ambassador.—" Three ; the most distant we call Tsgaru, the next Ara, and the nearest Niki. To the last belong these men here before us. They appear yearly with their tribute at the court of our king."

The Ruler of Tang.—" Does this land produce corn ? "

The Ambassador.—" No ; its inhabitants live on flesh."

The Ruler of Tang.—" Have they houses ? "

The· Ambassador.—" No ; they live in the mountains, under trunks of trees."

This extract is from the Nipponki, or Japanese Annals, from 661 until 696, which were collected in the year 720. They embrace thirty volumes octavo. The portions translated by Hoffman are to be found in vol. xxvi. p. 9; of Siebold's "Japanese Archives," viii. 130.

Since this time, in the seventh century, many wars have been undertaken against these northern border barbarians by their more civilised neighbours, and generally with success. But the inhabitants of Jeso always rose again after a short time, drove forth the Japanese invaders from the land, and gave themselves up again to their wild, original freedom, like their ancestors on the neighbouring island. Even at the present day the Japanese govern only a very small portion of Jeso, *i.e.*, the gold district of this remarkably rich island. Jeso readily leads to an acquaintance with Kamtschatka, which country was also described about the same period, in the following manner : [1]—

[1] *Vide* Steller's Description of Kamtschatka, Leipzig, 1734, p. 3. All that occurs here in quotation marks has been literally translated from the Year-Books of Tang (Tang-schu, bk. 220, p. 19, *v.*) The part not thus marked is drawn principally from Steller, and is added for explanation. The article of Mantuanlin (bk. 347, p. 5), may be compared with the Year-Books of Tang. The article is indeed evidently borrowed from the *Tang-schu*, but is much better arranged, and contains many original incidents, on which account I have freely availed myself of it. The compiler of the "Encyclopædia of Kang-hi" (*Juen-kien-hui-han*) satisfied himself (bk. 241, p. 19), as he frequently did, with merely transcribing from Mantuanlin.

KAMTSCHATKA IN THE TIME OF TANG.

Lieu-kuei (Loo-choo), or Hing-goci, as the Kamts-chadales of the present day term their fellow-country-men dwelling on the Penschinisch Bay, is situated, according to the Chinese Year-Books, fifteen thousand Chinese miles distant from the capital, which, according to the measurement of the celebrated astronomer Ihan, in the time of Tang, gives about three hundred and thirty-eight to one of our grades—the Chinese grades being rather smaller than our geographical. Now, Sigan, the capital of China during the dynasty of Tang, lies in the district Schensi, 34° 15′ 34″ north latitude, and 106° 34′ east longitude from Paris. Peter and Paul's Haven, on the contrary, according to Preuss, lies 53° 0′ 59″ north latitude, and 153° 19′ 56″ east longitude from Paris. These are differences which the accounts of the Chinese Year-Books establish in an astonishing manner, and leave no doubt whatever as to the identity of Kamtschatka with Lieu-kuei ; for it is certainly satis-factory if estimates of such great distances, drawn in all probability from the accounts of half-savage sailors or quite savage natives, should agree within two or three grades with accurate astronomic results.

" This land lies exactly north-east from the Black River, or Black Dragon River, and the Moko, and the voyage thither requires fifteen days, which is the time in which the Moko generally effect it."

The Moko here alluded to are, beyond doubt, the Mongolians, who governed in earlier ages, and even in the time of Tang as far south as Corea, and in the north as far as the other side of the Amur. The western limits of this people are unknown. In the east they dwelt, as our chronicle expressly remarks, as far as the ocean, or the Pacific, from whence they could very easily pass to the islands and to the American Continent. That this was in reality effected, is evident from their external appearance, as well as the affinity between the Mongolian language and that of the American Indians. The distance from Ocho-tock to the opposite peninsula is about 150 German miles, and, in fact, the natives generally require from ten to fifteen days to make the voyage.

" Lieu-kuei lies to the north of the North Sea,[1] by which it is on three sides surrounded. To the north this peninsula touches upon the land of Jetschay, or Tschuktschi, but the exact limits are not easy to determine ; it requires an entire month to make the journey from Kamtschatka to Jetschay. Beyond this the land is unexplored, and no mission has as yet come from thence to the Central Kingdom. Here are neither for-

[1] In Tang-schu an error of transcription occurs. Instead of Pe-hai, North Sea, we have Schao-hai, "little sea." The correct reading is to be found in the two encyclopædias already quoted. *Jetschaykno,* a kingdom, here " an excellent country ; " the Jetschay is only to be found in the encyclopædias. The arrogant Chinese love to write the names of foreigners with names which indicate scorn and contempt. Lieu-kuei, for example, signifies "the devil who runs through," and Jetschay, "the devil's companion."

tified places nor towns ; the people dwell in scattered groups on the sea-islands and along the shore, or on the banks of rivers, where they live by catching and salting fish.

Steller also assures us that the dwellings of the Itöl-men, or native Kamtschadales, are always situated on rivers, bays, or the mouths of the lesser streams, and especially in places which are surrounded by woods. Fish in incredible quantities, and in great variety, are found there, serving during the long winters as pro-vender for both men and cattle.   These they prepare in many ways, but principally by salting.   Those living still more to the north subsist almost entirely on the same food, from which they receive the name Eskimantik or Eskimo, *i.e.*, " raw-fish-eating."

" They dwell in caves, generally dug tolerably deep in the earth, around which they lay thick, unhewn planks."

This is applicable only to their winter dwellings ; their summer habitations are built high in the air, on posts like our dovecots.   The Itölmen dig out the earth to the depth of three or four feet in the form of a brick, and to such an extent as the number of their family may require.   The excavated earth they pile to the height of two or three feet around the pit thus formed, and then roof it with pieces of bark or willow sticks, five or six feet long, which they drive deep within the pit into the earth, so that the tops are all equally high.   Between these sticks and the earth they

B

generally lay dry straw, so that none of the earth may
fall through, nor any of the articles in the dwelling
become rusty or mouldy by direct contact with it; then
they leave a shelf of earth around, about a foot broad,
and lay great beams thereon in squares, which they
support on the outside with planks and sticks stuck
into the ground, so that they may not give way externally.   Then they place over them four posts cut in the
form of forks, as high as they wish to have the lodg-
ing in the middle.

Over this they lay again crosswise four beams, and
fasten them with thongs to the posts, upon which they
lay on every side the rafters.   Between these rafters
they put thin sticks, and across these small pieces of
wood, quite close together; this entire wooden roof
they cover to the depth of six inches with straw, shake
over it the remnant of the excavated earth, and tread
it down firm.   In the middle of the house they make
the hearth between four thin posts; of these posts,
two form the entrance, which is at the same time the
chimney.   Opposite the fireplace they dig out an air-
passage from eight to twelve feet long, according to the
size of the house, which passes beyond the limits of the
dwelling itself.   This is kept closed, except when they
are making a fire.   To facilitate the admission of air
they build the roof of the air-passage in such a manner
that the wind continually strikes against it, and is
drawn in.   If any one would enter, he must naturally
descend the door-chimney, which is done either by

means of a ladder, or the notched trunk of a tree. The smoky atmosphere is very oppressive to a European, though the natives support it without inconvenience. The little children generally creep through the draft, which also serves as a repository for cooking utensils. In the interior, cubes of wood are placed, to indicate the divisions of the separate sleeping-places.

" The climate, owing to fogs and heavy snows, is very severe. The natives are all clothed in furs, which they obtain by hunting. They also prepare a sort of cloth from dog's-hair and different species of grass. In winter they wear the skins of swine and reindeer; in summer, those of fish. They have great numbers of dogs."

We know that the climate of Kamtschatka presents remarkable differences. Districts situated at no great distance from each other have at the same season a different temperature. The southern part of the peninsula is damper, darker, and more exposed to terrible storm-winds, on account of its vicinity to the sea; but the farther north we ascend on the Pensinischen Bay, so much the milder are the winds in winter, and so much the less rain falls in summer. In no land are the fogs so frequent and so thick as in Kamtschatka, nor is any country known where deeper snows fall than between 51° and 54° of the peninsula. The natives, therefore, naturally require the heavy sea-dog (seal) and reindeer fur-clothing spoken of in the Chinese chronicle. The women prepare from dried nettles and other grasses a sort of linen which serves for all domestic purposes.

Reindeer, black bears, wolves, foxes, and other animals are found here in abundance, and are caught by a variety of ingenious methods, which the Chinese have also described. Dogs, which they use instead of horses to draw their sledges, are their only tame animals. It is an error of the Chinese writer when he speaks of swine; they would indeed succeed in this country, but in the time of Steller they were as yet unknown. Even at the present day several of the north-easterly Mantchou tribes clothe themselves in fish-skins, for which reason they are termed by the Chinese *Jupi*, or Fish-skins. These, like the Chadschen, belong to the Aleutes.

"The people have no regular constitution; they know nothing of officers and laws. If there is a robber in the land, all of the inhabitants assemble together to judge him. They know nothing of the divisions and courses of the four seasons. Their bows are about four feet long, and their arrows are like those of the Middle Kingdom. They prepare from bones and stones a sort of musical instrument; they love singing and dancing. They place their dead in the hollow trunks of trees, and mourn for them three years, without wearing any mourning-clothes. In the year 640, during the reign of the second Heaven's Son of Tang, came the first and last tribute-bringing embassy from the land of Lieu-kuei to the Middle Kingdom."

Before the conquest of their land by the Russians, the Kamtschadales lived in a sort of community, such as is generally found among all primitive tribes, as, for example, the early Germans. Every one revenged his own wrongs with the readiest weapons—such as bows, arrows, and bone-spears. In war they chose a leader whose authority ceased with it. In case of theft, where the offender was unknown, the elders called the people together, and advised them to give him up. When this proved unsuccessful, death and destruction were generally invoked upon his head by means of their Shamanic sorcery. They divide the entire solar year into summer and winter, but are ignorant of any division of time into days and weeks, and few are able to count above forty. They pass their time principally in dancing, singing, and relating tales and legends. Their songs and melodies, several of which are given in Steller, are remarkably soft and agreeable. "When I compare," says this excellent writer, "the songs of the great Orlando Lasso, with which the King of France was so much delighted after the Parisian Bloody Marriage, with these airs of the Itölmen, I am compelled, so far as agreeableness is concerned, to give the latter the preference." The Chinese account of the three years of mourning is groundless ; at least, when the Russians first discovered Kamtschatka, nothing of the kind existed. The sick were thrown, when beyond all hope of recovery, to the dogs, even while yet alive, and anything like mourning or lamenting from their surviving relatives was seldom even thought of. It is, however, possible, if not probable, that since the seventh century, the manners of the Kamtschadales have much changed, or deteriorated.

The situation of the Wen-schin, or Painted People, if we are to credit the account regarding their distance from Japan, must be sought for to the east of Kamtschatka, and within the Aleutian group of islands. "The land of Wen-schin," says the Year-Book of the Southern Dynasty, " is situated about 7000 Chinese miles (or twenty of our geographical degrees) to the north-east of Japan," [1] a direction and distance which places us in the midst of the Aleutian or Fox group of islands. It is not readily intelligible how Deguignes could seek and find these Painted People on the Island of Jeso.[2]

" Their bodies are usually covered with a variety of figures of animals and the like. On the forehead they have three lines : the long and straight indicate the nobles, the small and crooked the common people." [3]

The Aleutian or Fox Islanders, before their conversion to Christianity, not only cut, as is well known, a variety

[1] *Nausse, i.e.,* History of the Southern Dynasties, bk. 79, p. 5. The same article is to be found in *Leang-schu, i.e.,* in the Year-Book of Leang, bk. 54, p. 19, and by Mantuanlin, bk. 327, p. 2.

[2] Memoires de l'Academie des Inscriptions et Belles Lettres, xxxviii. 506. This is not the only error which this writer, so excellent in other respects, has made in this treatise.

[3] While engaged on this re-edition of Professor Neumann's work (London, March 1874), I have frequently seen two very curious Chinese figures, carved from wood, representing Aleutian Islanders. The faces are smooth, but the garment, or external figure, ingeniously adapted from some wood covered with a long fibre, gives them a very wild, hairy appearance.—C. G. L.

of figures upon the body, but also bored the cartilage
of the nose, and through it stuck a pin, upon which
they placed, on festive occasions, glass beads.   The
women, for a similar purpose, bored the ear.   Moreover, they made cuts in the under lip, in which they
wore needles of stone or bone, about two inches long.

CHAPTER III.

DURING the dynasty of Leang, in the first half of the sixth century, the Chinese often heard of a land situated 5000 of their miles to the eastward of the Painted People, who dwelt in the Aleutian Islands, and named it Tahan, or Great China. The direction and distance indicate the great peninsula Aliaska. They probably named it *Great* China from their having heard of the continent which extends beyond. It was in a precisely similar manner, according to the legend, that the Irish, who in earlier ages, long before the time of Columbus, were cast away on the American shores, named the country Great Ireland.[1] They reported that the newly-discovered nation altogether resembled the Painted People, but spoke an entirely different language. The Tahan bore no weapons, and knew nothing of war and strife.[2]

Beyond Aliaska the Chinese discovered, at the end of the fifth century, a land which Deguignes, in fact,

[1] Münchener Gelehrte Anzeigen, viii. 636. This must have been the land extending from the two Carolinas to the southern point of Florida.

[2] Leang-schu and Mantuanlin, *a. a. o.*

afterwards sought for on the north-west part of the American Continent. The conjecture of that keen-witted scholar was subsequently fully verified, and we are now able to determine those parts of America described by the Chinese. The zealous inquiries relating to a state of civilisation long passed away, and to such of its remains as yet exist in the New World, have led in our days to results of which the inquirer of the eighteenth century could have had no intimation. We will now give a literal translation of the Chinese report, and afterwards its explanation.

THE KINGDOM OF FUSANG, OR MEXICO.

" During the reign of the dynasty *Tsi*, in the first year of the year-naming, ' Everlasting Origin ' (A.D. 499), came a Buddhist priest from this kingdom, who bore the cloister-name of Hoei-schin, *i.e.*, Universal Compassion,[1] to the present district of Hukuang, and those surrounding it, who narrated that Fusang is about twenty thousand Chinese miles in an easterly direction from Tahan, and east of the Middle Kingdom. Many Fusang trees grow there, whose leaves resemble the *Dryanda cordifolia ;*[2] the sprouts, on the contrary,

[1] According to King-tschu it signifies "an old name." King-tschu is the sixth of the nine provinces which are described in the tax-roll of Ju, which contains the sixth of the included divisions of the Annual Book. It extended from the north side of the hill King. Compare Hongingta, the celebrated expounder of King in the times of Tang, with the already-mentioned extracts from the Annual or Year-Book.

[2] In the Leang-schu we find an error in the writing (a very common

resemble those of the bamboo-tree,[1] and are eaten by the inhabitants of the land. The fruit is like a pear in form, but is red. From the bark they prepare a sort of linen which they use for clothing, and also a sort of ornamented stuff." (With regard to this, the Year-Books of Leang have a variation : instead of the character KIN (11, 492 B.), meaning "embroidered stuff," or embroidered and ornamented stuff in general, we have MIEN, which signifies "fine silk.") "The houses are built of wooden beams ; fortified and walled places are there unknown."

OF WRITING AND CIVIL REGULATIONS IN FUSANG.

"They have written characters in this land, and prepare paper from the bark of the Fusang. The people have no weapons, and make no wars ; but in the arrangements for the kingdom they have a northern and a southern prison. Trifling offenders were lodged in the southern prison, but those confined for greater offences in the northern ; so that those who were about to receive grace could be placed in the southern prison, and those who were not, in the northern. Those men and women who were imprisoned for life were allowed to

occurrence in Chinese transcriptions) : instead of the character TONG (4, 233 Bas.), we have Tang (11, 444 B.), which signifies *copper*, and according to which we must read, "Their leaves resemble copper," which is evidently an error.

[1] This is the case also in China with the bamboo sprouts, on which account they are called *sun* (7, 449 B.) ; *i.e.*, the buds of the first ten days, since they only keep for that time.

marry.   The boys resulting from these marriages were,
at the age of eight years, sold as slaves; the girls not
until their ninth year.   If a man of any note was found
guilty of crimes, an assembly was held; it must be in
an excavated place." (*Grube*, Ger. "a pit;" possibly
within an embankment or circle of earth.—C. G. L.)
" There they strewed ashes over him, and bade him fare-
well.   If the offender was one of a lower class, he alone
was punished; but when of rank, the degradation was
extended to his children and grandchildren.   With
those of the highest rank it attained to the seventh
generation."

THE KINGDOM AND THE NOBLES OF FUSANG.

" The name of the king is pronounced Ichi.   The
nobles of the first-class are termed Tuilu; of the second,
Little Tuilu; and of the third, Na-to-scha.   When the
prince goes forth, he is accompanied by horns and
trumpets.   The colour of his clothes changes with the
different years.   In the two first of the ten-year cyclus
they are blue; in the two next, red; in the two following, yellow; in the two next, red; and in the last two,
black."

MANNERS AND CUSTOMS.

" The horns of the oxen are so large that they hold
ten bushels.   They use them to contain all manner of

things. Horses, oxen, and stags are harnessed to their
waggons. Stags are used here as cattle are used in the
Middle Kingdom, and from the milk of the hind they
make butter. The red pears of the Fusang-tree keep
good throughout the year. Moreover, they have apples
and reeds. From the latter they prepare mats. No
iron is found in this land; but copper, gold, and silver
are not prized, and do not serve as a medium of exchange in the market.

"Marriage is determined upon in the following manner:—The suitor builds himself a hut before the door
of the house where the one longed for dwells, and
waters and cleans the ground every morning and evening. When a year has passed by, if the maiden is not
inclined to marry him, he departs; should she be willing,
it is completed. When the parents die, they fast seven
days. For the death of the paternal or maternal grand-
father they lament five days; at the death of elder or
younger sisters or brothers, uncles or aunts, three days.
They then sit from morning to evening before an image
of the ghost, absorbed in prayer, but wear no mourning-
clothes. When the king dies, the son who succeeds
him does not busy himself for three years with State
affairs.

"In earlier times these people lived not according to
the laws of Buddha. But it happened that in the second
year-naming 'Great Light,' of Song (A.D. 458), five
beggar-monks from the kingdom of Kipin went to

this land, extended over it the religion of Buddha, and with it his holy writings and images. They instructed the people in the principles of monastic life, and so changed their manners."

AMAZONIA.

The same Buddhist monk who gives this account of the land Fusang, tells us of a country of women. "This land," he writes, " lies about a thousand Chinese miles in an easterly direction from Fusang, and is inhabited by white people with very hairy bodies." [1] The entire story is, however, intermixed with so much fabulous matter, that it is not worth translating. It is, however, worthy of remark, that since the earliest times every civilised race which has left us written records of its existence spoke of a land of women, which was always placed farther and farther to the north-east, until we find it ultimately placed in America. [2] It is hardly necessary to say that such a land of women could never have existed. It is, however, possible that among various tribes here and there the women may have had separate dwelling-places; perhaps apart upon an island, and held intercourse with the men only from time to time. The Arabs, particularly Edrisi, speak

[1] The reports are given in the Kansse, bk. 79, p. 5 ; Leang-schu, bk. 54, p. 49 ; and from these much more correctly in the Encyclopædia of Mantuanlin, bk. 327, *a. A.*

[2] The Japanese have in their *facetiæ* an account of such a country.— C. G. L.

of such an arrangement, but thought that this land of
women lay in an altogether different direction.[1] The
knowledge of the Arabs and Persians of the east and
north-eastern parts of the world extended only to Japan
and the eastern shores of China. " To the eastward
of Japan," asserts Abulfeda distinctly, " the earth is
uninhabited."

[1] Edrisi, ii. 433, edition Jaubert.

CHAPTER IV.

THE land west of the Indus, known to us at the present day under the names of Avghanistan and Beloochistan, was converted, shortly after the death of the Indian reformer Buddha, to his doctrine, which spread the system of castes, and was founded upon the principle of universal love.

It bears in the reports of the Chinese Buddhists the name Kipin, which appears in the different forms of Kaphen, Kaphes, and Kaphante, in the description of rivers and cities in Gedrosia and Arachosia by several of the older writers.[1] Here the third leader of the religion of the King's Son of Kapilapura had chosen his seat,[2] and here his disciples flourished in great power, as their numerous monuments and ruins indicate, until the seventh and eighth centuries, when the fanatic Moslem promulgated the doctrines of their own prophet with fire and sword.

[1] Mannert : Geographie der Griechen und Römer, v., Abtheilung ii. 19, 20, 53, und 55.

[2] *Vide* History of Buddhism, which bears the title *Tschi-jue-la, i.e.,* the Indian Guide, iii. 5, *v.*

To its holy city came many of the monks of Middle Asia
and China, and from Kophene again the religion extended itself to many parts of the world, even to North
America and Mexico.

How these American lands were named by their inhabitants we know not, as seems indeed to be generally
the case with most new discoveries of this nature.   We
know only that they received the name Fusang, which
was that of a tree common to these countries and
Eastern Asia, or, it would more probably appear, that of
an Asiatic tree resembling it in one or more particulars ;
for it seems to be a natural and usual circumstance
to name a newly-discovered land after some striking
peculiarity of the kind.   The Norsemen, who landed in
America five hundred years after these Buddhist priests,
named it in a similar manner Winaland—Wine or
Vine land—from the number of wild grapes which grew
there.   On account of the great distance of the land
Fusang, no missionaries went there afterwards.   And
yet the story of this land, so full of marvels, has not
yet disappeared from the memories of Chinese and
Buddhist inquirers into the wonders of the olden time.
Many of them have frequently mentioned it in their
works, and have even drawn maps of it,[1] and taken
the pains, in their thoughtless, unreflecting manner, to
collect all the accounts which we have here given.   Also,
at a later period, their mythical geographers and poets
often availed themselves of this piece of knowledge, and,

[1] *Fa-kiai-ngan-litu, i.e.,* More Certain Tables of Religion, i. 22.

as was the case in the West[1] with the land of Prester John, spun it out into all manner of strange tales. But these beautiful and romantic fancies about the land and tree Fusang can have no more weight with the impartial seeker into the truth of historical tradition than the legends of Alexander and of Charlemagne with the student of Arrian and Eginhard.[2]

The distance of the land from Tahan or Aliaska, which extends, according to the estimate before given, from the fifty-seventh to the fifty-eighth degree, leads us necessarily to the north-west coast of Mexico, and the vicinity of San Blas. Not less decisively do the Buddhist-Chinese reports indicate this part of the world. But before we can avail ourselves of these later accounts of the Aztecs, a difficulty must be removed, which would otherwise annihilate the complete mass of proofs.

THE OLDEST HISTORY OF MEXICO.

The information given by our Buddhist travellers goes back into times long anterior to the most remote periods alluded to in the obscure legends of the

[1] *Vide* Relation des Mongols ou Tartares, by the priest Jean du Plan de Carpin, Légat du Saint Siége Apostolique, &c., during the years 1245–47, given in the notice published by the Société de Geographie, under the above-mentioned title ; the travels of Sir John Mandeville, and Jacques de Vitry ; the works of Matthew of Paris, Joinville, Marco Polo ; and more particularly the old legend of Prestre Jehan, reprinted in "Le Monde Enchantée," par M. Ferdinand Denis, Paris, 1843, p. 184.—C. G. L.

[2] *Vide* Turpin's Chronicle, Warton ; "The Book of Legends," by O'Sullivan, Paris, 1842 ; also "The Romance of King Alisander," Weber's "Metrical Romances."—C. G. L.

Aztecs, resting upon uncertain interpretations of hiero-glyphics. One fact is, however, deeply rooted in this trembling soil of Old America : the races of barbarians which successively followed each other from the north to the south always murdered, hunted down, and sub-dued the previous inhabitants, and formed in course of time a new social and political life upon the ruins of the old system, to be again destroyed and renewed in a few centuries, by a new invasion of barbarians. The later native conquerors in the New World can, of course, no more be considered in the light of ori-ginal inhabitants than the present races of men in the Old World.

THE RUINS OF MITLA AND PALENQUE.[1]

The ruins named after the adjacent places, Mitla and Palenque, situated in the province Zzendales, near the limits of the municipality of Cuidad Real and Yucatan, have been supposed by enthusiastic scholars to possess an antiquity anterior, by thousands of years, to the coming of our Lord. Prejudiced and ignorant vision-aries have imagined this to be the home of all spiritual cultivation, and even to have discovered here traces of Buddhism. The Tolteks—a word signifying architects

---

[1] Antiquités Mexicaines, ii. 73, and Transactions of the American An-tiquarian Society, ii. On the subject of the early Mexicans, the reader may consult Prescott's "History of the Conquest of Mexico,"—a work as much distinguished by substantial erudition and critical tact, as by its simple, truly historical statements. (Ebenso ausgezeichnet durch gründliche Gelehrsamkeit und kritischen Tact, wie durch einfache ächt geschichtliche Darstellung.)—CARL F. NEUMANN.

—appeared about the middle of the seventh century, and one of their literary productions, known as " The Divine Book," existed, according to an unauthenticated legend, until the time of the Spaniards. The Aztecs, on the contrary, came to Anahuac, or " The Land near the Water," during the reign of Frederick the Second.[1] The savage invaders evinced at first the greatest hostility to the religion and social institutions of the conquered race, but feeling ultimately themselves the want of a regular system, they erected a new edifice upon the old ruins. This may prove advantageous in an intellectual or intelligent (*subjectiv*), as well as a material point of view, since we can thus avail ourselves of a knowledge of the laws, manners, and customs of the Aztecs, in order to obtain a clearer conception of the condition of the earlier races who inhabited this land.[2] The most learned historian of New Spain has already recognised in every particular, and in connection with the results of the most recent inquiries, the original affinity of the numerous Mexican languages.

The pyramidic-symbolic form of many of the Mexican monuments appears, indeed, to have a resemblance with the religious edifices of the Buddhists for places of interment ; but neither their architecture nor ornaments, according to Castañeda's drawings of Mexican antiquities, indicate any East Indian symbol, unless we

[1] The chronological accounts of the different authors contradict each other ; those of the learned Clavigero always appear to be the most correct.—PRESCOTT, i. ii.

[2] Clavigero, Storia Antica del Messico, i. 153.

are willing to admit their eight rings or stories as such.[1] According to a Buddhistic legend, the remains of Schakia were placed in eight metallic jars, and over these as many temples were erected.[2] But if Buddhism ever flourished in Central America, it certainly was not the pure religion of Schakia as it now exists in Nepaul, Thibet, and other parts of Asia, but a new religion, built upon its foundations. For the missionaries of Schakiamunis were in a manner Jesuits, who, the more readily to attain their aim, either based their doctrines upon, or intermixed them with, the existing manners and customs. The myth of the birth of the terrible Aztec god of war may possibly be a faded remain of the old Indian religion. Huitzilopotschli of Mexico was born in the same wonderful manner as Schakia of India; his mother saw a ball floating in the air, but one of shining feathers, placed it in her bosom, became pregnant, and gave birth to the terrible son, who came into the world with a spear in his right hand, a shield in his left, and a waving tuft of green feathers on his head. Juan de Grijalva, the nephew of Velasquez, was so much struck with the many instances of a high state of civilisation, and particularly with the magnificent buildings of Mexico, that he named the

---

[1] These circles suggest the eight rings of Odin, preserved in the eight arches of Norse towers. The ring of Odin produced every eighth night eight similar rings. It may be worth remarking in this connection, that the small pot-bellied phallic images in gold found in the graves of Central America, bear an extraordinary resemblance to a similar figure found in Ireland, and depicted on Etruscan vases.—C. G. L.

[2] Asiatic-Researches, xvi. 316.

peninsula New Spain, which term has since been extended to a much greater portion of the New World.

We know that the flora of the north-western part of
America is closely allied to that of China, Japan, and
other lands of Eastern Asia.[1] We may also assume that
the Fusang-tree was formerly found in America, and
afterwards, through neglect, became extinct. Tobacco
and Indian-corn seem always to have been as natural
to China as to the New World.[2] It is, however, much
more probable that the traveller described a plant
hitherto unknown to him, which supplies as many
wants in Mexico as the original Fusang is said to do
in Eastern Asia—I mean the great American aloe
(*Agave Americana*), called by the Indians " Maguey,"
which is so remarkably abundant in the plains of New
Spain. From the crushed leaves, even at the present
day, a firm paper is prepared. Upon such paper those
hieroglyphic manuscripts alluded to by the Buddhist
missionary, and destroyed by the fanatic Spaniards,
were written. From the sap an intoxicating drink is
made. Its large stiff leaves serve to roof their low
huts, and the fibres supply them with a variety of
thread and ropes. From the boiled roots they prepare
an agreeable food, and the thorns serve for pins and

[1] Prescott, i. 143.

[2] A very doubtful assertion, as regards tobacco. *Vide* communications
in " Notes and Queries for China."—C. G. L.

needles. This wonderful plant, therefore, provides them with food, drink, clothing, and writing materials; being, in fact, so fully satisfactory to every want of the Mexicans, that many persons, well acquainted with the land and its inhabitants, have asserted that the maguey-plant must be exterminated ere sloth and idleness, the two great impediments which hinder them from attaining a higher social position, can be checked.

METALS AND MONEY.

The use of iron, now found so plentifully in New Spain, was, as the Buddhist correctly remarked, unknown in Mexico. Copper and brass supplied its place, as was indeed the case at an early period in other countries. The natives prepared, according to Antonio de Herrera, two sorts of copper, a hard and a soft, the former of which was used to manufacture cutting tools and agricultural instruments, and the latter for pots and all manner of household implements. They understood the working of silver, tin, and lead mines; but neither the silver nor the gold which they picked up on the surface of the earth, or found in the beds of rivers, served as a circulating medium. These metals were not particularly prized in that land. Pieces of tin in the form of a common hammer,[1] and bundles of

[1] Do not these hammer-shaped Mexican coins bear a resemblance to the well-known shoe-shaped ingots of Sycee silver current in China? As regards the copper, recent discoveries indicate that it was brought by the Mexicans from the shores of Lake Superior. The highest northern traces of Mexican art and influence are, I believe, to be found in Tennessee.—C. G. L.

cacao containing a determined number of seeds, were the usual money.

LAWS AND CUSTOMS OF THE AZTECS.

The laws of the Aztecs were very strict, yet in the few remaining fragments of their hieroglyphical pictures we find no trace of the regulations of the land "Fusang." There existed, however, in the days of Montezuma, an hereditary nobility, divided into several ranks, of which authors give contradictory statements. Zurita speaks of four orders of chiefs, who were exempted from the payment of taxes, and enjoyed other immunities.[1]

Their method of marrying resembled that practised at the present day in Kamtschatka. We have no account of their mourning ceremonies, but know that the king had a particular palace in which he passed the time of mourning for his nearest relatives.[2] On the festivals of the gods they sounded horns and trumpets; this may have been done by the companions of the king, as to a representative of the godhead.[3]

The Aztecs reckoned according to a period of fifty-two years, and knew very exactly the time of the revolution of the earth about the sun. The ten-year cyclus spoken of in the Chinese report may have been a subdivision of the Aztec period, or have even been

[1] Prescott, i. 18. [2] Mithridates, iii. 33.
[3] Bernal Diaz : Historia de la Conquista, pp. 152, 153. Prescott, iii. 87, 97.

used as an independent period, as was the case with the Chinese, who term their notations " stems." It is worthy of remark that among the Mongols and Mantchous these " stems " are named after colours, which perhaps have some relation to the several colours of the royal clothing in the cyclus of Fusang.[1] These Tartaric tribes term the first two years of the ten-year cyclus " green and greenish ; " the two next " red and reddish,"[2] and so, in continuation, yellow and yellowish, white and whitish, and finally black and blackish. It appears, however, impossible to bring this cyclus of the Aztecs into any relation with those of the Asiatics, who universally reckon by periods of sixty years.

DOMESTIC ANIMALS.

The Aztecs had no beasts of draught or of burden. Horses were not found in the New World. The report of the Chinese missionary has, therefore, no connection with the later Mexican reigns. Two varieties of wild oxen with large horns ranged in herds on the plains of the Rio del Norte.[3] These might have been tamed by the earlier inhabitants, and used as domestic animals. Stag's horns have been found in the ruins of Mexican buildings ; and Montezuma showed the Spaniards, as curiosities, immensely large horns of this description.

[1] Gaubil : Observations Mathématiques, Paris, 1732, ii. 135.
[2] The second couple being termed red agrees with that of the Fusang cyclus.—C. G. L.
[1] Humboldt : Neuhispanien, ii. 138.

It is possible that the stags formerly ranged from New California, and other regions of North America, where they are still found in great numbers, to the interior of Mexico. To a native of China it must have seemed remarkable that the Mexicans should have prepared butter from hind's milk, since such a thing has seldom been done in China, either in ancient or modern times. When the inhabitants of Chusan saw the English sailors milking she-goats, they could not retain their gravity. It is indeed possible that the Chinese have described an animal similar to the horse with the character *Ma*, or horse, for changes of this nature are of frequent occurrence.[1] In such a manner many names of animals in the Old World have been applied to others of an entirely different nature in the New. The eastern limits of the Asiatic Continent are also the limits of the native land of the horse, and it appears that it was first taken in the third century of our era from Korea into Japan. But let the error in regard to the American horses have come from what source it will, the unprejudiced, circumspect inquirer will not be

[1] It is usual for all ignorant or unscientific people to give to animals for which they have no name that of some other creature with which they are familiar. Thus the gipsies speak of a fox as a *weshni juckal*, or wood-dog ; of an elephant as a *boro nakkescro gry*, or great-nosed horse ; of a monkey as a *bombaros*, and a lion as a *boro bombaros*, or big monkey, from their connection in menageries. Professor Neumann was probably ignorant of the fact, to which I allude more fully in another place, that the fossil remains of many horses found in America are of so recent a period, according to Professor Leidy, that they were probably coeval with man.—C. G. L.

determined on account of it to declare the entire story of Fusang-Mexico an idle tale. It appears to me that this description of the western coast of America is at least as authentic as the discovery of the eastern coast, as narrated in Icelandic sagas.

CHAPTER V.

CHINESE AND JAPANESE IN KAMTSCHATKA AND THE
HAWAIIAN GROUP.

A NUMBER of facts, taken from the occurrences of later
times, may be alleged to support the theory of a former
intercourse of China and Japan with the islands which
lie between those countries and America, and also with
the western coast of the latter. Even if the Chinese
and Japanese (to whom, with their knowledge of the
compass, such an enterprise would have presented no
difficulties) have never at any time intentionally undertaken a voyage to America, it has nevertheless happened that ships from Eastern Asia, China, and Japan,
as well as those of Russians from Ochotsk and Kamtschatka, have been cast away on the islands and coasts
of the New World.[1] The earliest Spanish travellers and
discoverers heard of foreign merchants who had landed
on the north-west coast of America, and even assert
that they saw fragments of a Chinese vessel.[2] This
much we know, that the crew of a Japanese junk acci-

[1] An account of a Russian ship cast away, A.D. 1761, on the coast of
California, may be found in the travels of several Jesuit missionaries in
America, published by Murr, Nuremberg, 1785, p. 337.

[2] Torquemada, Mon. Ind., iii. 7 ; Acosta, Hist. Nat. Amer., iii. 12.

dentally discovered a great continent in the East, remained there over winter, and safely returned home. The Japanese have remarked that the land extended further to the north-west.[1] They may have wintered in California, and then coasted as far north as Aliaska. Another Japanese vessel was wrecked about the end of the year 1832 on Oahu, one of the Sandwich Islands, concerning which the *Hawaiian Spectator* contained the following observation :[2]—" This Japanese vessel had nine men on board, who were bringing fish from one of the southern Chinese islands to Jeddo. A storm blew them out into the open sea, where they were driven about between ten and eleven months, until they finally landed in the haven Waiala, in the island Oahu. The ship was wrecked, but the men were brought safely to Honolulu, where they remained eighteen months, and then, by their own desire, were sent to Kamtschatka, whence they hoped to steal quietly into their own country; for the barbarously cruel Government of Japan,[3] mindful of the artifices of the Portuguese

[1] Kämpfer : Geschichte von Japan, Lemgo, 1777, i. 82.

[2] *Hawaiian Spectator*, i. 296, quoted in Belcher's "Voyage Round the World," London, 1843, i. 304. Also see "History of the Hawaiian or Sandwich Islands, from the earliest traditionary period to the present time," by James Jackson Jarvis, London, 1843. I have been personally well acquainted with both these writers, and can commend their works as those of men of accurate observation. Jarvis states that, according to the tradition of the islanders, several such vessels had been wrecked upon Hawaii before the island was discovered by whites or Europeans. —C. G. L.

[3] The reader will please to remember that all this was written thirty years ago, before Japan had entered on the great race of civilisation.

Jesuits, and continually fearing some plot on the part of the neighbouring Russians, have forbidden even the return of their own shipwrecked countrymen. As the natives of Hawaii," so continues the *Spectator*, " saw these foreigners, so similar to themselves in external appearance, and in many manners and customs, they were astonished, and declared unanimously, ' There is no doubt on the subject; we came from Asia.' " Another example of a Japanese vessel in America, and of the unreflecting, jealous policy of the Dairi, is as follows :— During the winter of 1833–34, a Japanese junk was wrecked on the north-west coast of America, in the vicinity of Queen Charlotte's Island, and the numerous crew, weakened by hunger, were murdered by the natives, with the exception of two persons. The Hudson Bay Company kindly took charge of these survivors, and sent them, in 1834, to England, whence they were forwarded to Macao. This was considered a fortunate event, and the English hoped that the Japanese Government, mindful of such kind treatment of their subjects, would show themselves grateful, and perhaps remove the restrictions against all foreigners. In vain. The ship that was to restore to the Japanese rulers their subjects, and at the same time aid in the missionary enterprise (Karl Gützlaff being on board), was received with a salute of cannon-balls, and obliged to leave, with unfulfilled intentions, the shores of this inhospitable land.

All of these facts show, however, and indeed sufficiently, that the passage of Eastern Asiatics to the western islands and shores of America is in the highest degree possible. And it is also possible that the inhabitants of these islands, in their weak boats, may from time to time, accidentally or intentionally, have landed upon the Asiatic Continent. "It is wonderful," says the Jesuit Hieronymus d'Angelis, the first European who landed in Jeso (A.D. 1618), "how bold and experienced are these people in the management of their vessels. In their frail boats they often undertake voyages of from two to three months' duration ; and however often they may be wrecked, still there are ever new adventurers ready to take their place and run the same risks."

THE FUTURE OF EASTERN ASIA.

The pride and barbarism of the numerous countries situated on the coasts of Asia and America, as well as of the inhabitants of the islands lying between, have forbidden hitherto any hope of a relation, commercial or otherwise, between them and the more enlightened world. Our age, however, which has broken through so many obstacles, never again to be closed, will ultimately break the chains of Eastern Asia, and give a world-movement (*Weltbewegung*) to the immense numbers imprisoned there. When this shall have been fully accomplished—and the beginning has already taken place—we can first hope for a regular, unbroken union between the Eastern and the Western World.

REMARKS

TEXT OF PROFESSOR NEUMANN.

CHAPTER VI.

SINCE the foregoing chapters were written, the author—my old friend and teacher—has passed away, and the prophecy with which his work ended has been singularly fulfilled. China is now thoroughly opened, and Japan, once proverbial for its exclusiveness, goes beyond more than one European country in her zeal to Europeanise. And I believe that time will show, when the records of these countries shall have been more carefully searched, that the same insight which induced Carl F. Neumann to prophecy the speedy opening of the East, was not at fault when he declared, on apparently slight data, his faith that in an early age the Chinese had penetrated Western America as far as Mexico.

It should be especially observed that, in commenting on the simple record of the old monk Hoei-Shin, Professor Neumann judiciously reminds the reader that the information given "goes back into a period long anterior to the most remote ages alluded to in the obscure legends of the Aztecs, resting upon uncertain interpretations of hieroglyphics." One thing we know, that in America, as in Asia or Europe, one wave of emigration

D

and conquest swept after another, each destroying in a great measure all traces of its predecessor. Thus in Peru the Inca race ruled over the lower caste, and would in time have probably extinguished it. But the Incas themselves were preceded by another and evidently more gifted race, since it is now known that these mysterious predecessors were far abler than themselves as architects. " Who this race were," says Prescott,[1] "and whence they came, may afford a tempting theme for inquiry to the speculative antiquarian. But it is a land of darkness, that lies far beyond the domain of history."

Problems as difficult, and far more unpromising, have, however, been solved within a few years, and entire literatures, histories, and languages have been exhumed, literally from the soil. Let me instance, for example, the earthen cylinders of Nineveh, of whose records it may not only be said, " Dust thou art, and to dust shalt thou return," but also, in the higher spirit of Christianity and humanity, " and from dust thou shalt rise again." *Nullæ latent, quæ non patent.* And there is a possibility that even in this secret of secrets, Old Peru, there lurks some slight possibility of elucidating the question of the Chinese in Mexico in the fifth century. For as the American waves of conquest flowed south, it is no extravagant hypothesis to assume that the race of men whom the monk encountered in " Fusang " may possibly have had something in common with what was

---

[1] Conquest of Peru, chap. I., i. 12, 13, edit. 1847. *Vide* note on page 60 of this work.

afterwards found farther south in the land of the Incas. One thing is certain, that there is a singularly Peruvian air in all that this short narrative tells us of the land Fusang. Fortified places, it says, were unknown, though there was evidently a high state of civilisation ; and yet this strange anomaly appears to have actually existed in ancient Peru, for Prescott speaks of the system of fortifications established through the empire as though it had originated with the Incas. Most extraordinary is, however, the remark of the monk that the houses are built with wooden beams. Now, as houses, all the world over, are generally constructed in this manner, the remark might seem almost superfluous. However, the Peruvians built their houses with wooden beams, and, as Prescott tells us, " knew no better way of holding the beams together than tying them with the thongs of *maguey*." Now, be it remarked that the monk makes a direct transition from speaking of the textile fibre and fabric of the maguey to the wooden beams of the houses—a coincidence which is at least striking, though it be no proof. It is precisely as though he had the maguey in his memory, and were about to add it to his mention of the wooden beams. And we may notice that this construction of houses was admirably adapted to a land of earthquakes such as Southern America, and that Prescott himself testifies that a number of them " still survive, while the more modern constructions of the conquerors are buried in ruins."

Most strikingly Peruvian is the monk's account of
the kingdom and the nobles.   The name Ichi is very
like the natural Chinese pronunciation of the word *Inca*.
The stress laid on the three ranks of nobles suggests
the Peruvian Inca castes of lower grade, as well as the
Mexican ; while the stately going forth of the king,
" accompanied by horns and trumpets," vividly recalls
Prescott's account of the journeyings of the Peruvian
potentate.   The change of the colour of his garments
according to the astronomical cycle is, however, more
thoroughly in accordance with the spirit of the institutions of the Children of the Sun than anything which we
have met in the whole of this strange and obsolete record.
And it is indeed remarkable that Professor Neumann,
who had already indicated the southern course of Aztec
or of Mexican civilisation, and who manifested, as the
reader may have observed, so much shrewdness in adducing testimony for the old monk's narrative, did not
search more closely into Peruvian history for that confirmation which a slight inquiry seems to indicate is by
no means wanting in it.   Thus, with regard to the
observation of the seasons, Prescott tells us that " the
ritual of the Incas involved a routine of observances
as complex and elaborate as ever distinguished that of
any nation, whether pagan or Christian."   Each month
had its appropriate festival, or rather festivals.   The
four principal had reference to the sun, and comme-
morated the great periods of his annual progress, the
solstices and equinoxes.   Garments of a peculiar wool,

and feathers of a peculiar colour, were reserved to the Inca. I cannot identify the blue, red, yellow, and black (curiously reminding one of the alchemical elementary colours still preserved by a strange feeling for antiquity or custom in chemists' windows), but it is worthy of remark that the rainbow was the Inca's special attribute or scutcheon, and that his whole life was passed in accordance with the requisitions of astronomical festivals ; and the fact that different colours were reserved to him, and identified with him, is very curious, and establishes a strange analogy with the narrative of Hoei-shin.

I would, however, specially observe on this subject of the cycles and changes of colours corresponding to astronomical mutations, that Montesinos[1] expressly asserts that the Peruvians threw their years into cycles of ten—a fact which has quite escaped the notice of Neumann, who conjectures that the decade of Fusang may have been a subdivision of the Aztec period, or even have been used as an independent one, as was indeed the case with the Chinese, who termed these notations "stems." "It is worthy of remark," he adds, " that among the Mongols and Mantchous these ' stems ' are named after colours, which, perhaps, have some relation to the several colours of the royal clothing in the cycles of Fusang. These Tartaric tribes term the first two years of the ten-year cyclus, green and greenish,

[1] Montesinos : Memorias Antiquas, MS., lib. ii. cap. 7. *Vide* Prescott's Conquest of Peru, bk. i. p. 128.

the next red and reddish, and so on, yellow and yellowish, white and whitish, and finally black and blackish."[1]

Peru, certainly, is not Mexico; but I would here recall my former observation that Mexico *might* have been at one time peopled by a race having Peruvian customs, which in after years were borne by them far to the south. The ancient mythology and ethnography of Mexico present in their turn a mass of curious, though perhaps accidental, identities with those of Asia. And both Mexico and Peru had the tradition of a deluge from which seven prisoners escaped. In the hieroglyphs of the former country, these seven are represented as issuing from an egg.

We may note also that a Peruvian tradition declares the first missionaries of civilisation who visited them to have been white and bearded. "This may remind us," says Prescott, "of the tradition existing among the Aztecs in respect to Quetzalcoatl, the good deity, who, with a similar garb and aspect, came up the great plateau from the east, on a like benevolent mission

---

[1] Mr Hyde Clarke has pointed out, in some remarks to which I shall again have occasion to refer, that there are many curious circumstances as to the use of colours in connection with numbers; and that, for instance in many of the prehistoric languages, the word for *red* and that for the number two were identical. Very little can be inferred from this, and nothing can be based upon it, but the coincidence, though slight, is curious, and may serve as a basis for future observation. Red, it may be remarked, is the *second* colour in the Fusang cyclus as mentioned by Hoei-shin. In the symbolism of the Roman Catholic Church, blue and white are identified in the Pope, but the Cardinals next him, or the second rank, wear *red*. Red, as I have already indicated, was the colour both of the second Tartar and second Fusang couple of years in the cyclus.

to the natives." In the same way the Aesir, Children of Light, or of the Sun, came from the east to Scandinavia, and taught the lore of the gods.

The Peruvian embalming of the royal dead takes us back to Egypt ; the burning of the wives of the deceased Incas reveals India ; the singularly patriarchal character of the whole Peruvian policy is like that of China in the olden time; while the system of espionage, of tranquillity, of physical well-being, and the iron-like immovability in which their whole social frame was cast bring before us Japan—as it was a very few years ago. In fact, there is something strangely Japanese in the entire cultus of Peru as described by all writers.

It is remarkable that the Supreme Being of the Peruvians was worshipped under the names of Pachacomac, " He who sustains or gives life to the universe," and of Viracocha,[1] " Foam of the Sea," a name strikingly recalling Venus Aphrodité, the female and second principle of life in many ancient mythologies. Not less curious (if authentic) is the tradition of the Vestal Virgins of the Sun, who, it is said, were buried alive if detected in an intrigue, and whose duty it was to keep burning the sacred fire obtained at the festival of Raymi.

> " Vigilemque sacraverat ignem
> Excubias divûm æternas."

This fire was obtained, as by the ancient Romans, on

[1] To-day in Peru white men are called Viracochas. "Myths of the New World," by D. G. Brinton, M.D., New York, 1868, p. 180.

a precisely similar occasion, by means of a concave mirror of polished metal.[1] The Incas, in order to preserve purity of race, married their own sisters, as did the kings of Persia, and of other Oriental nations, urged by a like feeling of pride, and possibly in accordance with a faith in the physical law set forth a few years ago in the *Fortnightly* and the *Westminster Reviews.* Among the Peruvians, *mama* signified mother, while *papa* was applied to the chief priest. "With both, the term seems to embrace in its most comprehensive sense the paternal relation, in which it is more familiarly employed by most of the nations of Europe."

It has been observed that, as in the case of the Green Corn Festival of the Creek Indians of Georgia,[2] many striking analogies can be established between the Indian tribes of North America and the Peruvians. Gallatin has shown the affinity of languages between all the American aborigines. It is possible that the first race which subsequently spread southward, may with modifications have occupied the entire north.

Let the reader also remember, that while the proofs of the existence or residence of Orientals in America are extremely vague and uncertain—and I trust that it

[1] The Liang-sze-kung-ki says that envoys from Fusang to China brought, as tribute, square and circular mirrors more than a foot in circumference. These were called "gems for observing the sun"—possibly metallic burning-glasses. *Vide* "Notes and Queries for China and Japan," 1870.

[2] *Vide* "The Green Corn Dance," from an unpublished MS. by John Howard Payne, author of "Home, Sweet Home," in the *Continental Monthly.* Boston, 1862.

will be borne in mind that this admission has been made sincerely and cheerfully—and while they are supported only by coincidences, the *antecedent probability* of their having come hither, or having been able to come, is stronger than the Norse discovery of the New World, or even than that of Columbus himself would appear to be. Let the reader take the map of the Northern Pacific; let him ascertain for himself the fact that from Kamtschatka, which was well known to the old Chinese, to Aliaska, the journey is far less arduous than from China proper, and it will be seen that there was in all probability abundant intercourse of some kind between the continents. In early times, the Chinese were bold and skilful navigators, to whom the chain of the Aleutian Islands would have been simply like stepping-stones over a shallow brook to a child. For it is a well-ascertained fact, that a sailor in an open boat might cross from Asia to America by the Aleutian Islands in summer-time, and hardly ever be out of sight of land, and this in a part of the sea generally abounding in fish, as is proved by the fishermen who inhabit many of these islands, on which fresh water is always to be found. Nor when in Aliaska would the emigrant from Asia be deterred, during half the year at least, by the severity of the climate. If the country be not, as the late Mr Seward was jocosely said to have declared, abounding in pine-apples and polar bears, icebergs and strawberries, it is at least tolerably habitable, as I know by the testimony of several friends—

one of whom even wintered out there while searching for gold — and from a Russian - English newspaper published in that remote country. From a number of this newspaper, containing the advertisement of books published by Nicholas Trübner of London, I infer that a very fair degree of luxury, not devoid of erudition, may now be attained in Aliaska. In short, to an enterprising Buddhist monk, inspired with the zeal of a missionary, this journey to Fusang does not present one half the difficulties which thousands of exactly such monks undergo at the present day in their journeyings over the vast and sterile plains and through the hostile mountain ranges of Central Asia. I have, indeed, no doubt that, even as I write, there is living, travelling, and preaching, more than one such Eastern Cordelier, bearing literally the very name of Hoei-shin, whose journeyings have been as wide, as wild, and as weary as those of him who long ago returned and told, like King Thibault of Navarre, his story of lands beyond sea—

> " Outre mer j'ay fait mon pélerinage,
>   Et souffert ay moult grande dommage,"

—and so passed away to a quiet cloister grave. The bedesman sleeps among his ashes cold, little thinking, before he died, that more than a thousand years after his story had been told it would rise again thousands of miles away, and go, for men to read, even in Tahan itself.

Seriously enough, the only real marvel as regards the

probability of the Chinese having been in Mexico thirteen hundred years ago would be that they were never there, and did not make the journey. When we see a nation, as China once was, with a religious propaganda, sending missionaries thousands of miles beyond its borders ; boasting a commerce, and gifted with astronomers and geographers of no mean ability, we must certainly believe that it made many discoveries. And when we find its pioneers advancing for centuries in a certain direction, chronicling correctly every step made, and accurately describing the geography and ethnography of every region on the way, we have no ground to deny the last advance which their authentic history claims to have made, however indisposed we may be to admit it. One thing, at least, will probably be cheerfully conceded by the impartial reader, that the subject well deserves further investigation, which it will obtain from those students who are occupied in exploring the mysteries of Oriental literature and the archæology of both worlds.

NOTE TO CHAPTER VI.

I would not be understood as intimating that the civilisation of Fusang was simply Peruvian. Some of the peculiarities observed by Hoei-shin—as, for example, the manner of wooing, the exposure of the dead, and the possible origin of his Kingdom of Women—existed in a strongly-marked form among the Red Indians; others recall New Mexican or Aztec culture, as it may have been ere driven south; and there are, withal, Siberian-Mongolian traces. But I cannot resist the feeling, which has grown on me through years of study on this subject, that in the fifth century the Buddhist monk visited a race combining characteristics and customs which afterwards spread to the south and east. All that he observed is singularly American, and, from the tone of the narrative, was evidently new to the missionary. Since Prescott wrote, many investigators have declared that the civilisation once attributed entirely to the Incas, was derived by them from earlier races which they had supplanted. Thus Thomas J. Hutchinson ("Two Years in Peru, by T. J. Hutchinson, F.R.G.S., &c.," London, 1873) tells us that the Chincas preceded the Yuncas, and that the Yuncas were conquered by the Inca Pachacutec so recently as the fifteenth century of our era. Tradition also gives the names of several races as preceding the Chincas in Peru. It is, however, conjectured that, whatever the race may have been which occupied Peru, it took from its predecessors culture which they in like manner had inherited. In endeavouring to find some analogy between Fusang as described by Hoei-shin, and Peru as described by Prescott, I by no means consider that the customs attributed to the Incas were unknown before their time.

LETTER

FROM

COLONEL BARCLAY KENNON

ON THE

NAVIGATION OF THE NORTH PACIFIC OCEAN.

CHAPTER VII.

IT will naturally have occurred to the reader that the strongest proof which can be alleged in favour of the journey of Hoei-shin and his Buddhist predecessors to the Continent of North America is the demonstration of the ease with which it could be performed. This has indeed been largely shown by Professor Neumann, and I am happy in being able to state that more recent researches have thrown additional light on this very curious question. While writing the last pages of the foregoing chapter, I was so fortunate as to meet in London with Colonel Barclay Kennon, who is personally and practically familiar with every step which Hoei-shin and his mysterious five predecessors must have taken, he having been the navigating-officer in the North Pacific, China Seas, and Behring's Straits, of the United States North Pacific Surveying Expedition, 1853–56, Lieutenant John Rodgers commanding. This gentleman was so kind as to take an interest in my work, and obligingly communicated to me, in a letter which I subjoin, such facts as he could recall in reference to Professor Neumann's verifications. I trust that it will not be out of place for me to state that Colonel Kennon, a graduate of Annapolis Naval Academy, United States of America, was the first person who ever made a cast of the lead for the first Transatlantic cable, October 4, 1852, and in 1857 was, as Lieutenant of the United States Navy, navigating-officer of the ship *Niagara*, by which the first Atlantic cable was laid— although it cannot be denied that, as is the case with too many beginnings, it came to grief. After the Civil War, Lieutenant Kennon entered the Egyptian service as Colonel. He is the inventor of the well-known Counterpoise Battery, for the protection of artillery in coast defence, and was decorated by the Khedive for the construction of a fort on this principle.

It should be borne in mind that, as regards the passage of the short distances between Asia and America by the Aleutian chain, where one is out of sight of land for a very short time, the vessels of North-eastern Asia were formerly built for long voyages and oceanic navigation, and actually did sail for weeks together out on the open sea; that the compass was probably used by them before the fifth century, and that at the present day Japanese vessels are still rigged in a much more sea-going style than Chinese junks, and are consequently capable of easier and more extended navigation.

The evidence offered in favour of the discovery of America by the Chinese Buddhists of the fifth century is very limited, but it has every characteristic of a serious State document, and of authentic history. It is distinctly recorded among the annals of the Empire. At the time these journeys were undertaken, thousands of monks, inspired by the most fanatical zeal, were extending their doctrines in every direction; and this they did with such success, that though Buddhism has now been steadily declining for many centuries, it still numbers more followers than Christianity, or any other religion on the face of the earth, for they are literally counted by hundreds of millions. And as their doctrines urged propagandism, it would be almost a matter of wonder if some of the missionaries of the faith had not found their way over an already familiar route.

LETTER *from* COLONEL BARCLAY KENNON, *formerly of the United States North Pacific Surveying Expedition.*

"LONDON, *April* 3, 1874.

" DEAR SIR,—As regards the possible passage at an early age of Chinese to the North American Continent, I regret to say that I have devoted too little thought to such a subject to be of use to you, beyond giving a fair idea of the distances between point and point from China to Japan, and thence, *via* the Kurile and Aleutian Islands, to the Western Coast of America. I have at present unfortunately no map, chart, or notes to guide me or refresh my memory, and so must depend solely upon it. Thus far, however, it has not misled me in other respects, and it certainly should not in this case, if it be considered that I was the sailing-master of the

E

surveying schooner which was specially appointed to
follow, examine, and map out this route.

" After leaving Shanghai direct for Japan, a vessel
sights Alceste Island when about 200 miles from the
mouth of the Yang-tse-kiang, upon a branch of which
river, the Woo-sung, Shanghae is situated.   From Alceste Island to the Gotto Islands, which are directly upon
the Japanese coast, and two miles from its extreme
western end, the distance is about 120 miles.   In
making this trip, a fair wind, with ' plenty of it,'
will very soon take a vessel from point to point.
The distance across from one point on the Chinese
coast is still shorter, or about 100 miles S.S.E.
from the Yang-tse-kiang.   Many islands lie off
this point, which, being lost sight of at a distance
of twenty or more miles, will materially diminish the
time for being in the open sea.   In fact, no ordinary
Chinese or Japanese fisherman would hesitate to make
these trifling voyages for so short a time out of sight
of land, and hundreds do make much more dangerous
ventures every day along the coast.   From the Yang-
tse-kiang direct to the coast of Korea the distance is
less than a day's sail, or only eighteen hours by
coasting it, till we reach the Straits of Korea, when a
few hours take us over to the Straits of Krusenstern,
separated by islands, and thence direct to the Gotto
Islands.   Or we may sail for the island of Oki, and cross
the straits (which received in our survey, and on our
map, the name of Rodgers' Straits), which are from ten

to twenty miles wide, and thus reach the coast of Japan. In either case, land is not long lost sight of, the open sea distances being very trifling.

" Starting from Hong Kong Island, farther south, a run of thirty-six hours takes us to the island of Formosa. To the eastward of it, and in sight from each other, are the Madjico Sima Islands, and to the eastward of them are visible those of Amakirima. In full view with these, again, the southernmost of the Loo-choo Islands, dependencies of Japan, of which Shapa is the capital, heaves in sight. Running north through this group to the coast of Japan, one island is hardly below the horizon before another makes its appearance, or in a very few hours, the last being in sight when close to the south-west end of Niphon, the largest of the Japanese Islands. These latter lie N.E. and S.W. ; so that by following either coast-line until the Kuriles are reached, land will always be in sight. The Kurile Islands, stretching between the island of Matsumai (the northernmost of the Japan group, and upon which Hakododi, the chief port and town, is situated), and Cape Lapatka, the southern extremity of Kamtschatka, are in sight from each other, excepting possibly in the ' Boussole Passage,' which is forty or more miles in width. A vessel in the centre of it will have the islands marking its boundaries in sight; so that as soon as the voyager passes from one land, he immediately perceives the other. Kamtschatka, once seen, is not easily lost sight of, as its high mountains are visible for more than a hundred miles. The highest peak, just north of Avataka Bay, containing the harbour and remains of the town of Petropaulski, is a volcano ; and, if my memory does not mislead me, it is more than 18,000 feet in height, the line of perpetual snow beginning some distance below the crater, and terminating at a point some thousands of feet above the sea-level. This line, of course, offers a mark which can be seen farther out at sea than would a mountain of the same height, if entirely covered up to its summit. Proceeding along this coast to Cape Kronotski, which lies north of Petropaulski, the distance to Behring's Island is about 150 miles—course, east. Fifteen miles only from it is Copper Island, and about 150 miles southwest of it is Attou Island, the most westerly of the Aleutian group, which is an almost unbroken chain, connecting with the American Continent at the peninsula of Aliaska.

" Attou Island, situated in latitude 53° N., longitude 173° E. (in round numbers), has the pretty little harbour of Tchitchagoff, which we surveyed with much care, believing that it might prove useful at some future day. Owing to the trouble and care with which this work was done, the three islands standing off its entrance were named after the vessel, *Cooper ;* the captain, Gibson ; and myself. It may not be out of place to state, that the schooner *Fenimore Cooper* was originally a small New York pilot-boat of seventy-five tons, and that for two years in these stormy Northern Seas I spent a happy life on board of, and sailed upwards of 40,000 miles in her. After leaving New York she went to Africa, Java, China, Japan, California, and back to Japan, where she finally ' laid her bones to dry.'

" Next to Attou Island, and close to it, is Agattou and Semichi ; and before losing sight of either of them, Boulder Island, distant forty-five miles from Agattou, heaves in sight. Kusha, the Island of the Seven Moun-tains—all of which are volcanoes, either extinct or active—and Amtchitka come next. These are the Krysi or Rat Islands. Next to Amtchitka, in the Andranof group, is Tonago, volcanic, Adakh, Atkha, and Ammnak, with other smaller islands between them, all in sight one from the other. Adakh has a fair harbour for small vessels, but is not inhabited. We were three weeks there. In Atkha there is a not inconsiderable settlement, and good anchorage. Here we found a Greek priest, whose wife, a Georgian, was really beautiful, as were their two daughters. At this time the Russian War was at its height, and the supplies of these poor people being exhausted, and themselves in great dis-tress, we found it a great pleasure to relieve them—particularly the ladies, who were the first we had seen for many months. I need not say how delighted they were to receive a good stock of sugar, coffee, tea, medicines, and ' canned fruit.'

" Between Ammnak and Unalashka are, I believe, eight islands. This group bears the name of the Fox

Islands. The whole chain, from Attou to Unalashka inclusive, is called the Aleutians, the easternmost of which is very near the American mainland, or peninsula of Aliaska. A few of these islands are inhabited, the people bearing a strong resemblance to the Kuriles, who, in turn, are like the Nootka Sound Indians,[1] whose country is on the mainland to the eastward of the peninsula of Aliaska, but which may actually be reached either in a vessel or *on foot* by following the coast-line.

"You wish to know if I can adduce any proofs or probabilities that during the great period from the fifth to the seventh centuries, when the world was so abundantly busy in making converts to its several religions, Buddhist priests passed by these islands. If they did, they certainly could not have remained long in them, and must have hurried to the more hospitable shores of America. For there is literally not a tree on these islands—in fact, nothing resembling one, unless I except a few very small bushes, the tallest not more than three feet high, with no branches larger than a man's finger. From Aliaska a vessel could take the roundabout course of following the coast-line to reach

[1] I have verified by many inquiries the assertion that there is a continuous line of likeness between the natives from the North-west Coast of America to the Asiatic Continent. "I find myself more and more inclined to believe," says John D. Baldwin, in his "Ancient America," . . . . "that the wild Indians of the north came originally from Asia, where the race to which they belong seems still represented by the Koraks and Cookchees found in that part of Asia which extends to Behring's Straits."—C. G. L.

Sitka; but a run of three or four days would, with a good breeze, make the trip on a much more direct course—and likewise a more sensible one—by running down among the islands of the group in which Sitka is situated.

" From this place Vancouver's Island is soon reached; that is to say, in three or four days, with land in sight nearly every hour of the time. Oregon is but a few hours' sail after this ; and by keeping in with the land, any lubber of a navigator can *see* his way down the coast to Cape Saint Lucas, the southern end of California, which is distant about 200 miles west of Mazatlan, Mexico. The prevailing winds are from the northward, or from the north-westward, with a current (*Kuro-suvo*) setting to the southward. Vessels bound down the coast, to the southward, make the run quickly by keeping just outside the influence of the land-breezes; while those bound *up* the coast should profit by them by sailing near the land. A small vessel, being able to run close in, could anchor when the sea-breezes set in during the day, but should lift her anchor at night, to make her *northings* with those from the land.

" From what I have written, and from the result of the most accurate scientific observation, it is evident that the voyage from China to America can be made without being out of sight of land for more than a few hours at any one time. To a landsman, unfamiliar with long voyages, the mere idea of being 'alone on the wide, wide sea,' with nothing but water visible, even

for an hour, conveys a strange sense of desolation, of
daring, and of adventure.   But in truth it is regarded
as a mere trifle, not only by regular seafaring men, but
even by the rudest races in all parts of the world ; and
I have no doubt that from the remotest ages, and on
all shores, fishermen in open boats, canoes, or even
coracles, guided simply by the stars and currents, have
not hesitated to go far out of sight of land.   At the
present day, natives of many of the South Pacific
Islands undertake, without a compass, and successfully,
long voyages which astonish even a regular Jack-tar,
who is not often astonished at anything.   If this can
be done by savages, it hardly seems possible that the
Asiatic-American voyage was not successfully performed by people of advanced scientific culture, who
had, it is generally believed, the compass, and who
from an early age were proficient in astronomy.

" But though this voyage from the oldest portion
of the Old World—historically speaking—to the newest
portion of the New, can be made by remaining almost
constantly in sight of land, I do not recommend it ;
and I am sure that any man in any kind of a boat,
who had sufficient enterprise and patience to undertake
it, would have easily found the shorter route.   But
there is a still stronger argument for the voyage across
having been undertaken, in this, that Chinese sailors
had long been travelling in a route of which this was a
mere continuation, and that not a very difficult one.
For, in reality, from Singapore in Malacca to Batavia

in the island of Java, and to Shanghai in China, the trip is almost an actual coasting one, the steamers nowadays running from point to point. To a landsman it is doubtless pleasant to see fresh islands every day, but a sailor greatly prefers the open sea, until he makes the land near his port. From Hakododi, Japan, the arc of the great circle joining it with San Francisco passes almost exactly beside the central island of the Aleutians. This distance is about 4250 miles. One objection to the route is this, the fogs about those islands being actually ten times worse, in every way, than those of London, they are avoided as much as possible by steering farther south, or rather by running more directly to the east. I may mention in this relation, that I had a Kamtschatka dog on board the schooner, and found him more useful as a " look-out " than a shipload of sailors could have been, since they could have done literally nothing, while the dog seemed strangely attracted towards the land, and when *smelling* it, invariably stood with his head towards it, barking aloud, so that we were more than once thereby warned of its too close proximity.

" We have on our own coast, or that of the United States of North America, the Gulf Stream, which, flowing off to the eastward, and striking the shores of Europe, falls on them, and on those of Africa, down to about the equator, then running west to the coast of South America, passes its northern shores up through the Carribean Sea to between Yucatan and Cuba, and renews its course through the Straits of Florida, and again up our coast. Now in the North Pacific there is another stream, called the Kuro-suvo, or Japanese Current, which, passing up the south-east side of the Japanese coast, flows off to the eastward until it reaches California; then running down that coast, and that of Mexico and Central America, to latitude 10° N. (more or less), meets the Peruvian or Humboldt Current, when both bear away to the west and form the *Northern* Equatorial Current, which, extending to the Ladrone Islands, in latitude 18°, longitude 145°, turns towards the northernmost of the Lorchas Islands, and finally completes the circuit on the coast of Japan. It is much like the Atlantic Gulf Stream in many particulars, and its current is quite as strong in certain places, though the water in it is not so warm. This current is of great utility to vessels bound to the eastward, its counter-current being of course of corresponding advantage to those sailing westward.

" From what I know of the track across from Asia to America, and from what I have seen of the Japanese and Chinese, I have no doubt whatever that from very early times they occasionally visited our American shores. Assuming that they took the route which I have described, they would have been constantly in sight of land; and there is something in the nature and appearance of the frequently-recurring islands which would naturally tempt farther exploration, and lead them on. The weather is, it is true, cold at Behring's Straits even in summer, but not one-fourth so cold as at Matsumai, Japan, in winter. A Japanese vessel, running up the Kamtschatka coast to the Bay of St Lawrence in Siberia, would have, at the utmost, only a day's sail, but probably less, to reach America; and by going that distance farther north, her crew could see land across Behring's Straits through the whole passage during the summer season, it being then free from ice, with an open sea and a moderate degree of cold. Nothing is more likely than that such visits were made by fur-hunters in former years; and as so many foreign countries lay within such easy sailing distance, it is probable that the Chinese and Japanese Governments—especially the latter—issued edicts for the building of all vessels upon a model which should very much limit their navigation, and confine them to short cruises.

" Few would believe, who are familiar with the Portuguese of the present day, or with their marine, that this people once supplied the adventurous navigators who found their way to India by the way of the Cape of Good Hope ; and yet it is less than three hundred years since Vasco di Gama made that famous cruise. He coasted, as the records of the voyage show, and as the time spent would of itself prove ; and it is quite likely that Chinese and Japanese did the same thing until the sterns of their vessels were ' stove in ' by order of their Governments, to restrict them to cruising nearer home.

" Columbus had a very different kind of work to do,

for during the long cruise of many weeks which he spent at sea, he saw nothing whatever until the end of his journey. Two of his vessels were much larger than the little schooner in which I sailed so many thousands of miles, and the Japanese junks with which I am familiar were generally five times larger, and with eight times the capacity of the little *Fenimore Cooper*. There is certainly no reason why they could not keep the sea as long as any other vessel. Columbus had ' caravels,' which were more or less open, but this is not the case with the Japanese junks, which are entirely closed.

" It is of some importance in this connection to observe, that when surveying the coast of Japan in 1854, I found the Japanese charts to be invariably very correct ; their latitudes, which came directly from observations of the heavenly bodies, being particularly so. Their longitudes, of course, did not agree with ours, for we were ignorant of their starting-point or primary meridian. The relative bearings and distances of places one from the other, with the outlines of the coast, were singularly accurate.

" The Japanese have doubtless very often made involuntary voyages of much greater extent, and far more dangerous, than this from continent to continent. In 1849, when I was in the Sandwich Islands, I learned that an American whaler had picked up a Japanese junk about 2300 miles south-east of Japan, and had sent her people to China on board a passing vessel, from which country they doubtless found their way back to their home. And I can distinctly remember that five years ago, and two years since also, Japanese junks were found among the Aleutian Islands, having been drifted thither by the Kuro-suvo Current, and impelled by westerly gales of wind. One was picked up on Adakh, which is nearly half-way over to San Francisco. Had these vessels been supplied with provisions, with such a trip in view as that of crossing the Pacific, there was nothing whatever to prevent their making it to and fro. In 1854 and 1855, when I was last in Japan, I often saw both women and children on board junks in which they had been to the Loo-choo Islands. Those I met with in the latter islands seemed to be as much the habitual homes of their owners and families as are the Chinese river-boats homes to those who inhabit them. In China one sees many families which have for generations been born and reared on board these little boats. And at present the actual floating population on the Canton river alone is estimated at over a million of souls.

" I have always regarded the Sandwich Islanders as cousins of the Japanese. There is quite enough in the general appearance of the two races to justify one in believing it. To me it seems as if some other blood existed there, very largely mingled or alloyed with Japanese, and the difference in manners, customs, religion, and other forms of culture, is owing to the Japanese element being in the minority. But suppos-

ing them to have altogether descended from the
Japanese, and this is far from being improbable,[1] the
few who first landed there, and from whom the whole
group was peopled, found, in organising, voluntarily or
involuntarily, a new form of government and new institutions, no more necessity to copy after their old
types than did the early settlers of America in framing
theirs.   In fact, if they were exiles, like the first settlers
of Iceland and many other countries, their natural impulse would be to avoid forming anything like the
tyranny from which they had fled or were banished.
The Japanese have always had a highly-organised religion, while the Sandwich Islanders had as nearly none
as was possible, and the melancholy history of their
degradation and decay under European culture seems
to indicate that they are incapable of receiving any.
As to the difference or non-existence of customs, we
have only to go to any of the ' new countries ' of the
present day to see that the so-called habits and peculiarities of mankind, which once gave such interest to

---

[1] It is a well-established fact, and one within my own observation, that
the children of Irish parents in America, even in the first generation, change
materially from the ancestral Celtic type. This is especially remarkable
in the girls, even when born and bred in the backwoods. The face becomes
more oval, and the eyes darker (when not Galwegian, or naturally dark),
and softer in expression. The pure, unmixed Pennsylvania German stock
retain the broad shoulders and heavy figure of their ancestors ; but the
hair is generally much darker, and the eyes, which are often very beautiful,
are, as in the Irish instance, larger. The same holds good, but in a less
degree, I believe, of the children of English parents. The child of
" Boston people," born in New Orleans, often becomes in the first generation a creole, pale, sallow, and with constantly cold hands.—C. G. L.

elementary works on geography, are everywhere vanishing as guides to help one in tracing the origin of races ; in fact, if civilisation at the present day, unlike the ancient, were not accompanied by the spirit of anti-quarian research, and a passion for recording all that it learns, the past would soon vanish as regards all races without a written history. The differences in the mode of life, and in many other things, between the United States and England, are very marked. The Loo-chooese also vary in many respects from the Japanese, although their islands are in sight of each other, and the former are dependencies of the latter. Napa-kiang, in Loo-choo, is built of stone, while all the large Japanese cities are of wood. Again, the manner of dressing the hair varies entirely in these provinces, a matter which, while small in itself, constitutes a very serious difference in a race with which such trifles are of almost radical importance. The Loo-chooese and Japanese are the same people, but they build their houses differently, simply because one country abounds in wood and the other in stone ; and the difference in the arrangement of the hair has doubtless been determined by some law of climate, or caprice on the part of a ruler either in fashion or politics—the two being in this country generally combined.

"The islands of the Pacific are remarkably alike, both as regards size and general appearance ; and as Oceanica is to the *leeward* of Japan, and the resemblance between their respective populations has occurred to every sailor who has been in the two countries, it is a very rational conclusion that these places have been settled from the mainland by mariners blown out of their course. Such mishaps occur every two or three years at the present day, and such have occurred for hundreds, and it may be for thousands, of years. The ancient and confirmed habit of both Japanese and Chinese, of taking women to sea with them, or of traders keeping their families on board, would fully account for the population of these islands, even if they had been originally deserts. We have only to suppose the same impulses and causes acting in the more easily-travelled eastern direction, along the Aleutian chain, in seas abounding with fish and easily navigable, to conjecture whether such adventurers, voluntary or involuntary, ever reached America from Asia. The mere resemblance of immense numbers of North American Indians to the so-called Mongolian tribes is a sufficient answer to such a question. Respectfully and truly yours,

" BARCLAY KENNON."

CHAPTER VIII.

REMARKS ON COLONEL KENNON'S LETTER.

THE letter from Colonel Kennon, and more particularly
the argument for the settlement of Oceanica from Japan,
are links in the chain of circumstantial evidence, showing
that in all probability the inhabitants of Eastern Asia
once passed to Western America. I myself have seen
Sandwich Islanders of the best class, well-educated—
occupying, in fact, the position of ladies and gentlemen—
who were not to be distinguished by me from the same
class of Japanese, only that the Sandwich Islanders
seemed to be rather the better-looking. Some of the
Pacific islands are even now uninhabited, which renders it the more probable that those which are not
derived their population from the country which lies,
as Colonel Kennon remarks, " to the windward."
Taking everything therefore into consideration, the
scientific character of early Chinese and Japanese navigation, the crowded state of the empires, which, despite
stringent laws, continually compelled thousands to
either live on the water, or seek a living by voyaging;
the islands thousands of miles away which were pro-

F

bably peopled by them, and the great ease with which
the journey by the Aleutian Islands could be accomplished, we have a chain of inductions which require
only the least fact to establish the whole as truth.
This fact is *probably* to be found in the record of the
journey of Hoei-shin.   All that now remains is the
hope that, if curiosity and inquiry should be stimulated
by the publication of what is here given, further research may be made in China, or in its ancient records,
for clearer evidence.   I have heard it said that it is
commonly related by the Chinese in California that
their ancestors had preceded them by many centuries
in that country, which tradition was once recorded in a
San Francisco newspaper.   This may have originated
in some obscure version of the old story of Hoei-shin,
but then it is not impossible that there are sources of
information extant on this subject which were never
known to Europeans.

As regards the discovery of America by the Norsemen, while there is apparently good direct evidence to
establish what is now (popularly, at least) regarded as a
fact, the chain of general and presumptive evidence is
not so strong as that which indicates the probable
transit of Chinese or Japanese to Aliaska.   It is true
the Icelanders were dauntless seamen and reckless
adventurers, and that the passage to Greenland presented no great difficulty to them.   But all these
conditions existed equally as regards seamanship, and
to a much higher degree as to the ease of the journey,

for Japanese or their neighbours. Scandinavia and Iceland were never at any time more than thinly populated ; but the teeming millions of Eastern Asia have in all ages been proverbial. It is certainly true that one fact is worth all the presumptive evidence which can be imagined ; and it is equally true that the least fact is entitled to peculiar consideration and respect when heralded and supported on every side by probabilities.

There is a class of very unscientific writers on many subjects, but especially on Ethnology, who affect a negative method in everything, and ridicule every new thing as belonging rather to the realm of fairy tales than to science. With these writers nothing was ever derived from a strange source, or could have come from anything of which they were ignorant. This tendency is not inspired by truth, but by that timidity rather than prudence which dreads failure or ridicule, and contents itself with theorising and arranging in the track of bolder minds and true discoverers. Opposition to or belief in what they regard as " religion," has also much to do with this spirit of denial, since many, and indeed far too many writers, are guided in every department of science by a desire to prove or disprove Christianity, rather than to find out what is true. To them all the extraordinary coincidences of serpent-worship, monolithic groups, cups, winged globes, or crosses in monuments, are merely phenomena of an accidental nature, and the most natural things in the world, such as must have occurred to everybody. In philology they are identical with that very large class of unthinking and generally uneducated people who deem it useless to seek for the origin of cant words or popular phrases, so convinced are they that such " catches" come spontaneously to people's lips. " Everybody uses them, so they must have come of themselves to everybody," said a man of this class once to me. " A man can't help saying them." Now, as much research in this field has convinced me that every popular saying has a *decided* origin, popular belief to the contrary, it seems most probable that such very positive matters as religions and myths, which are difficult to learn, are, with the customs which they involve, more generally transmitted, however remotely, than easily invented. A snake is a singular object, and its motion on the ground is very much like the winding course of a great river, and the island or islands so generally found in the delta of a river naturally suggest something held in the mouth of the snake; and yet I do not think that the idea of a serpent with a ball at its mouth is so very palpable a religious symbol, and one so innate, that it should be the very first thing which would occur as an emblem of the great deity of the waters, to aboriginal Egyptians, to monolith-setters in Brittany, to mound-builders in Ohio, to Peruvians and Mexicans. In fact, I deem it not altogether impossible that this poetical collocation of the serpent as a type of a river, and the ball, simple and self-suggesting as it is, has never occurred to many of my readers. It would be preposterous to deny what Sir John Lubbock has all but proved in "The Origin of Civilisation," that many methods of worship have occurred independently and spontaneously to savage races widely remote one from the other. Yet, on the other hand, few impartial investigators will deny that *transmission* has also been a wonderful element in what Germans call *culture.*

If Buddhist priests were really the first men who, within the scope of written history and authentic annals, went from the Old World to the New, the fact is of great value in itself, and one which must doubtless lead the way to much important knowledge as to all the early settlement or culture of Old America. And if it be a fact, it will sooner or later be proved. Nothing can escape History that belongs to it. Within a generation Egypt and Assyria have yielded the greatest secrets of their language and life to patient inquiry; every week at present sees the most wonderful conquests, from the dreamy realm of myth and fable to that of material record and fact. I do not know how or when it will be, but I am persuaded that ancient America will in time yield her Moabite stones and Rosetta slabs to the patient inquirer. The records of Mexico were carefully destroyed by wicked bigots, who, not satisfied with exterminating a flourishing and happy nation, sought to commit a double murder by killing its past life. But it will be found again; for science will yet achieve that, and more.

CHAPTER IX.

PERHAPS the strongest link in the chain of circumstantial evidence which can be adduced to prove that Hoei-shin and others penetrated to California and Mexico, is one which has been almost neglected by Professor Neumann, so lightly does he touch upon it. I refer to the zeal with which Buddhist monks wandered for centuries forth from China, through regions so remote, and among perils of so trying a nature, that the journey of Hoei-shin and of his predecessors seems, when we study the route, and allow that they probably travelled in summer, comparatively a pleasure-trip. The result of these missionary enterprises was fortunately a large collection of published "Voyages and Travels," several of which are still extant. Of late years the interesting nature of these works has caused the translation of several of the more important into European languages; and of these I propose to make some slight mention, supposing that a little account of such writings would be acceptable, as bearing on the character of the first discoverers

of America. For, little as we have of the record of
Hoei-shin, its general resemblance to that of the other
Buddhist missionary travellers is so striking, that no
one can fail to detect a marked family likeness.

Chief in the work of translation from these journals
is the celebrated Chinese scholar Stanislas Julien, whose
versions of Buddhist travels into French fill over 1500
octavo pages. From these works it is evident that it
was a special matter of pride among those missionaries
to excel their predecessors in the extent of their
journeys, and in the zeal or success with which they
distributed the doctrines and sacred images of Buddha.
References to these sacred images abound in Buddhistic works, indicating that immense numbers must
have been carried to all places where the missionaries
penetrated. One of these works of pious adventure is
the very interesting " History of the Life of Hiouen-
thsang, and of his Travels in India, from the year
629 to 645. Followed by documents and geographical
explanations, drawn from the original narrative. Translated by Stanislas Julien, Member of the Institute of
France, &c. Paris, 1853."

" From the fourth century of the Christian era to the
tenth," says Julien, " the Chinese pilgrims who went
into the countries west of China, and particularly into
India, to study the doctrine of Buddha, and bring back
the books containing it, have published a great number
of narratives, itineraries and descriptions, more or less

extended, of the countries which they visited. . . . .
Unfortunately the greater part have perished, unless
they remain buried in some obscure convent in China."
Thus we cannot sufficiently regret the loss of "The
Description of Western Countries," by Chi-tao'-an,[1] a
Chinese Shaman, who became a monk in 316, and consequently preceded Fa-hien, who did not go forth until
the year 339 of our era. But the loss most to be
regretted is, unquestionably, "The Description of
Western Countries, in Sixty Volumes, with Forty Books
of Pictures and Maps," which, edited in accordance with
an Imperial decree, by many official writers, after the
memoirs of the most distinguished religious and secular
authors, appeared in the year 666, with an introduction written by the Emperor Kao-thsang, the cost being
defrayed by Government. This work was entitled,
in the original Chinese, Si-yu-tchi-lou-chi-kouen, Hoa-
thou-sse-chi-kiouen ("A Description of the Western
Countries, in Sixty Books, with Forty Books of Illustrations and Maps," as above). M. Stanislas Julien
was apparently not aware that a copy of this work was
kept in the Royal Palace at Pekin, as any book written,
though only in part, by an Emperor, would naturally
be, in accordance with Chinese custom. It was, however, unfortunately burned in the "looting" of the
Summer Palace, in which perished such masses of valu-

[1] Chi-tao'-an-si-yu-tchi.   *Vide* the Cyclopædia Youen-kien-louai-han,
published in 710, bk. cccxvi. p. 10 ; and the life of this priest in Ching-
seng-tch'ouen, bk. ii. p. 1.

able historical and literary material, never to be re-
covered. This work has been called a description of
the Chinese Empire, but from the exact account of
it which has been published, it was evidently the one
spoken of by Julien. In fact, a carefully-detailed description of the Chinese Empire in the seventh century,
fully illustrated, must have been in great part quite
the same as "A Journey to the West," and it is not
likely that two works of such magnitude, and on almost
the same subject, were published contemporaneously at
such enormous expense as they must have involved.
"It would be worth while," Julien continues, "for the
Catholic missionaries who live near Nankin to seek for
this work in the valuable library of that city, where my
friend, the late Mr Robert Thom, former British Consul,
discovered, and persuaded me to copy, ten years ago,
232 volumes in quarto, of texts and commentaries,
which for centuries were to be found no longer in any
other Chinese library. At present there are only six
works of this kind—*i.e.*, Buddhist travels—in the
original text, and duplicates of these are to be found
in France and Russia. Their names and dates are as
follows :—

I. Memoir of the Kingdoms of Buddha. Edited by
Fa-hien, a Chinese monk, who left the Kingdom of the
West in the year 399 of our era, and visited thirty
kingdoms.

II. Memoir of Hoei-seng and of Song-yun, envoys to

India in 518, by order of the Empress, to seek for sacred books and relics.

III. Memoirs of Western Countries. Edited in the year 648 by Hiouen-thsang. This work was written originally " in the language of India. It embraces a description of one hundred and thirty-eight kingdoms ; although, according to a Chinese authority, Hiouen-thsang had only been in one hundred and ten." The extraordinary number of countries visited by this missionary, and his manifest desire to make his travels appear as extended as possible, give a strong colour of probability to the assertion that these monks went wherever they could, and explored the remotest regions, deterred by no dangers. Since they brought the religion of Buddha to distant places in Siberia, as the curious black Buddhistic books from that country now in St Petersburg prove, and to Kamtschatka and the Aleutian Islands, nothing is more probable than that such zealous propagandists should have gone a step beyond, and have arrived in a part of the North American Continent where reports of Aztec or other civilisation must have lured them still farther on.

IV. History of the Master of the Law of the Three Collections of the Convent of Grand Benevolence. This work, the first editing of which was by Hoei-li, continued and edited by Yen-thsang, both contemporaries of Hiouen-thsang, contains the history of his remarkable journey, accompanied by very interesting biographical details wanting in the original narrative.

V. The History and the Journeys of Fifty-six Monks of the Dynasty of Thang, who went to the West of China to seek the Law.

VI. The Itinerary of the Travels of Khi-nie.

It is worth noting that the authenticity of the great work of Hiouen-thsang, which has been impugned by one or two European writers, has been triumphantly vindicated by M. Julien. And there can be no doubt, that in every instance these journeys were carried out to the end proposed, and that the books are *bona fide* narratives. They are as authentic as the accounts of modern Episcopal, Presbyterian, Methodist, or other missionaries. It is true that, like Hoei-shin or Herodotus, these monks often narrate extravagant miracles and marvels as they heard them ; and it may be that they lend too ready a faith to them—as did Sir John Mandeville, and most early travellers. But where they said they had been, they had gone. This is apparent enough. And there is no reason for rejecting the story of Hoei-shin, any more than that of his contemporaries, because he narrates hearsay wonders.

Another very interesting work of this school, which will be found more readily accessible to my readers than the somewhat rare and costly translations of M. Julien, is " The Travels of Fah-hian, from 400 to 415 A.D.," and " The Mission of Sung-yun." Both of these were Buddhist pilgrims from China to India, and their two books, rendered into English by Samuel Beal, have been published in one volume by N. Trübner, 57 Ludgate Hill, London. Of the character of these works, something may be inferred from the motto taken from the life of Gaudama, by the Right Rev. P. Bigandet, Vicar-Apostolic of Ava and Pegu, who declares, " It is not a little surprising that we should have to acknowledge the fact that the voyages of two Chinese travellers, undertaken in the fifth and seventh centuries of our era, have done more to elucidate the history and geography of Buddhism in India than all that has hitherto been found in the Sanscrit and Pali books of India and the neighbouring countries." This is very strong testimony as to the general accuracy of observation and truthfulness of the Chinese Buddhist travelling monks, two of whom were probably contemporary with Hoei-shin, and these he may have seen at the court of the Empress Dowager Tai-Hau of the Great Wei dynasty, who favoured such missionaries, sending them afar to advance the faith. It is far from unlikely that men so celebrated for the extent of their travels, and occupied with precisely the same pursuits, should have met and exchanged their experiences. For Hoei-seng and Song-yun, who travelled only nineteen years after Hoei-shin, were, as we know, celebrated in their time, their journal having been published by command of an Empress. Therefore it is improbable that Hoei-shin was less celebrated in his time at a court and in a country where travellers and books of travel were, as we have seen, duly appreciated, since an Emperor deigned to write the introduction with his own Imperial hand to the book of one Buddhist missionary monk, and then had it published in the most magnificent manner at his own expense. We may well call a work magnificent, the fame of which has endured for fourteen hundred years, and must the more deeply regret its wanton destruction by ignorant and reckless soldiers.

The credibility or importance of one of this class of books is naturally enough upheld by that of the rest, and the narrative of Hoei-shin, viewed in this light, acquires additional probability. It is to be regretted that Professor Neumann should have omitted as unimportant, or as detrimental to the authenticity of his text, that " fabulous matter " which, he assumes, is not worth translating. Absurd fables occur abundantly in the travels of Hoei-shin's contemporaries, as in those of Herodotus ; but being merely given as reports, their very existence may serve to establish an identity of style with that of writers whom no one at the present day regards as untruthful. The study of these Buddhist travels will convince the reader that their authors were singularly alike in their caste of mind and manner of observation, but unquestionably honest. They are as simple as Saxon monks, whom they greatly resemble : all their thoughts and phrases are distinct units.

It may be observed that Colonel Kennon's last remark in his letter is in reference to the " resemblance of immense numbers of North American Indians to the so-called Mongolian tribes." This resemblance has often been remarked by Americans. I was recently indebted to the kindness of the Hon. Charles D. Poston, late Commissioner of the United States of America in Asia, for a work written by him entitled, " The Parsees," which includes observations in India, Japan, and China. In this book, the only comparison made as to similarity of races is the following, in an incident which took place " beyond the Great Wall : "—

" A Mongolian came riding up on a little black pony, followed by a servant on a camel, rocking like a windmill. He stopped a moment to exchange panto-mimic salutations. He was full of electricity, and alive with motion ; the blood was warm in his veins, and the fire was bright in his eye. I could have sworn that he was an Apache ; every action, motion, and look re-minded me of my old enemies and neighbours in Ari-zona. They are the true descendants of the nomadic Tartars of Asia, and preserve every instinct of the race. He shook hands friendlily but timidly, *keeping all the time in motion like an Apache.*"

I have italicised these last words, since they indicate great familiarity with the Apaches, as well as the shrewd observation which is characteristic of the writer. All Indians do not closely approach this type, nor do all Tartars. But it is not to be doubted that among the " Horse-Indians " great numbers have a peculiarly Mongolian expression, often approaching to identity, as if there were a common blood, which, when developed in nomadic life on Asiatic steppes and Western American prairies, had produced cognate results. This resemblance is so strong, that most readers will be tempted to inquire if there are any signs of philological affinity connecting these races. What I have been able to ascertain, which is also due to the researches of one whom I have known personally for many years, will be found in the following chapter.

AMERICAN ANTIQUITIES,

WITH THEIR

RELATIONS TO THE OLD WORLD.

THE DAKOTA LANGUAGE AND THE URAL-ALTAIC
TONGUES—THE MOUND-BUILDERS—
IMAGES OF BUDDHA.

CHAPTER X.

A VAST amount of research and ingenuity has been employed in establishing resemblances between the archæological remains of Mexico and those of Central America and Peru, and the temptation to transfer many of the assumed proofs or arguments to these pages is naturally very great. I have, however, resisted it, partly because this material is accessible to all who are interested in the subject of the possible origin of the American races, and partly because so much of it is unscientific and fanciful, that a degree of discredit rests upon it. Many remarkable facts exist; but in truth, they exist thus far, like the record of Hoei-shin, rather as an incentive to further research than as clearly-defined historical monuments. A remark recently made by Mr Hyde Clarke, when officiating as chairman at a meeting of the Society of Arts,[1] has, however, suggested to me some investigations by a learned German, well known to me personally, which I shall not scruple to reproduce, as they are

[1] April 15, 1874. *Vide Journal of the Society of Arts*, April 17, 1874. It was in commenting on a lecture on the " Symbolism of Oriental Ornament," delivered by William Simson, F.R.G.S., that the remark in question was made.

appropriate to the subject of an affinity between Old
America and Asia.   On this occasion Mr Clarke said
that the " subject was so vast, it was impossible to deal
thoroughly with it ; but he might mention, that only
recently some of the monuments in the Indo-Chinese
Peninsula—in Cambodia and Pegu—had been found by
himself to greatly resemble in form those of Mexico
and South America ; and, at the same time, strong
affinities were discovered between the languages.   He
had just discovered, also, that there was affinity between
the Akkad form of the earliest cuneiform inscriptions
(which remained even now almost without interpretation)
and the Aymara, in Peru, thus establishing one historic
chain from ' Babylon to the New World.'[1]   New facts
were constantly coming forward, and they all tended to
illustrate the same interesting and important doctrine
—the unity which there had always been in the human
race, and the way in which progress had been carried
onwards from one generation to another, for the building up of a system of civilisation which, when properly
applied, would contribute to the benefit of all."

It was the reference by Mr Clarke to the resemblance
between American and Asiatic languages which reminded
me of some comments by the distinguished linguist
F. L. O. Roehrig, who, as the discoverer of a group of

---

[1] As I have not examined this subject, I know nothing of these affinities.
I quote Mr Clarke's remarks on account of their general bearing on American languages, and as an introduction to another writer.   The existence of
ancient inscriptions in Peru is, I believe, as yet doubtful.

new tongues in Central Asia, and as the author of an " Essay on Languages," to which was awarded the prize of the French Institute, is entitled to respect, the more so as his views are quite free from anything visionary or fanciful. In a monograph " On the Language of the Dakota or Sioux Indians," published in 1872 at Washington, "from the Report of the Smithsonian Institution," he speaks as follows :—

" So far as we know, the Dakota language, with several cognate tongues, constitutes a separate class or family among American-Indian languages. But the question at present is, Whence does the Dakota, with its related American tongues, come? From what trunk or parent stock is it derived? Ethnologists are wont to point us to Asia as the most probable source of the prehistorical immigration from the Old World. ' Hence,' they say, ' many, if not all, of our Indians must have come from Eastern or Middle Asia ; and in considering their respective tongues, one must still find somewhere in that region some cognate, though perhaps very remotely-related, set of languages, however much the affinity existing between the Indian tongues and these may have gradually become obscured, and in how many instances soever, through a succession of ages, the old family features may have been impaired. But they further allow, of course, that these changes may have taken place to such an extent that this affinity cannot be easily recognised, and may be much, even altogether, obliterated.

" When we consider the languages of the great Asiatic Continent, of its upper and eastern portions more particularly, with a view of discovering any remaining trace, however faint, of analogy with, or similarity to, the Dakota tongue, what do we find? Very little ; and the only group of Asiatic languages in which we could possibly fancy we perceived any kind of dim and vague resemblance, an occasional analogy, or other perhaps merely casual coincidence with the Sioux or Dakota tongue, would probably be the so-called 'Ural-Altaic' family. This group embraces a very wide range, and is found scattered in manifold ramifications through parts of Eastern, Northern, and Middle Asia, extending in some of its more remote branches even to the heart of Europe, where the Hungarian and the numerous tongues of the far-spread Finnish tribes offer still the same characteristics, and an unmistakable impress of the old Ural-Altaic relationship.

"In the following pages we shall present some isolated glimpses of such resemblances, analogies, &c., with the Sioux language as strike us, though we need not repeat that no conclusions whatever can be drawn from them regarding any affinity, ever so remote, between the Ural-Altaic languages and the Dakota tongue. This much, however, may perhaps be admitted from what we have to say, that at least an *Asiatic origin* of the Sioux or Dakota nation and their language may not be altogether an impossibility.

"In the first place, we find that as in those Ural-Altaic languages, so in a like manner in the Sioux or Dakota tongue, there exists that remarkable syntactical structure of sentences which we might call a constant inversion of the mode and order in which *we* are accustomed to think. Thus, more or less, the people who speak those languages would begin sentences or periods where we *end* ours, so that our thoughts would really appear in their minds as inverted.

"Those Asiatic languages have, moreover, no prepositions, but only *post*positions. So, likewise, has the Dakota tongue.

"The polysynthetic arrangement which prevails throughout the majority of the American-Indian languages is less prominent, and decidedly less intricate, in the Dakota tongue than in those of the other tribes of this continent. But it may be safely asserted that the above-mentioned languages of Asia also contain, at least, a similar polysynthetic *tendency*, though merely in an incipient state, a rudimental or partially-developed form.

Thus, for instance, all the various modifications which the fundamental meaning of a verb has to undergo, such as passive condition, causation, reflexive action, mutuality, and the like, are embodied in the verb itself by means of interposition, or a sort of intercalation of certain characteristic syllables between the root and the grammatical endings of such a verb, whereby a long-continued and united series, or catenation, is often obtained, forming, apparently, one huge word. However, to elucidate this further here would evidently lead us too far away from our present subject and purpose. We only add that postpositions, pronouns, as well as the interrogative particle, &c., are also commonly blended into one with the nouns, by being inserted one after the other, where several such expressions occur in the manner alluded to, the whole being closed by the grammatical terminations, so as often to form words of considerable length.[1] May we not feel authorised to infer from this some sort of approach, in however feeble a degree, of those Asiatic languages —through this principle of catenation—to the general polysynthetic system of the American tongues ?

" We now proceed to a singular phenomenon, which we should like to describe technically, as a sort of *reduplicatio intensitiva.* It exists in the Mongolian and Turco-Tartar branches of the Ural-Altaic group, and some vestiges of it we found, to our great surprise, also in the language of our Sioux Indians.[2]

" This reduplication is, in the above-mentioned Asiatic languages, applied particularly to adjectives denoting colour and external qualities, and it is just the same in the Dakota language. It consists in prefixing to any given word its first syllable in the shape of a reduplication, this syllable thus occurring twice—often adding to it (as the case may be) a *p*, &c.

" The object—at least in the Asiatic languages alluded to—

---

[1] Such intercalations are, in a measure, almost analogous to the usual insertion of the many incidental clauses in long Latin or German sentences, if we are allowed that comparison.

[2] This *reduplicatio intensitiva* is not uncommon in Hindustani.—C. G. L.

is to express thereby in many cases a higher degree or increase of the quality. An example or two will make it clear. Thus we have, for instance, in Mongolian, *khara*, which means black; and KHAP-*khara*, with the meaning of very black, entirely black; *tsagan*, white, TSAP-*tsagan*, entirely white, &c.; and in the Turkish and the so-called Tartar (Tatar) dialects of Asiatic Russia, *kara*, black, and KAP-*kara*, very black; *sary*, yellow, and SAP-*sary*, entirely yellow, &c.

" Now in Dakota we find *sapa*, black, and with the reduplication SAP-*sapa*. The reduplication here is, indeed, a reduplication of the syllable *sa*, and not of *sap*, the word being *sa*-pa, and not *sap*-a. The *p* in SAP-*sapa* is inserted after the reduplication of the first syllable, just as we have seen in the above, *kara* and KAP-*kara*, &c.

" In the Ural-Altaic languages *m* also is sometimes inserted after the first syllable; for instance, in the Turkish *beyaz*, white, and BEM-*beyaz*, very white, &c. If we find, however, similar instances in the Dakota language, such as *ćepa*, which means *fleshy* (one of the external qualities to which this rule applies), and ćEM *ćepa*, &c., we must consider that the letter *m* is in such cases merely a contraction, and replaces, moreover, another labial letter (*p*) followed by a vowel, particularly *a*. Thus, for instance, *ćom* is a contraction for *ćopa*, *ġam* for *ġapa*, *ham* for *hapa*, *skem* for *skepa*, *om* for *opa*, *tom* for *topa*, &c. So is *ćem*, in our example, only an abridged form of *cepa*; hence *m* stands here for *p* or *pa*, and belongs essentially *to the word itself*, while in those Asiatic languages the *m* is *added* to the reduplication of the first syllable, like the KAp in p-*kara*, &c. We have therefore to be very careful in our conclusions.

" The simple doubling of the first syllable is also of frequent occurrence in Dakota; for instance, *ġi*, brown, and *ġiġi* (same meaning); *sni*, cold, and *snisni*; *ko*, quick, and *koko*, &c.

" There are also some very interesting examples to be found in the Dakota language which strikingly remind us of a remarkable peculiarity frequently met with in the Asiatic languages above adverted to. It consists in the *antagonism* in *form*, as well as in meaning, of certain words, according to the nature of their vowels; so that when such words contain what we may call the strong, full, or hard vowels—viz., *a, o,* or *u* (in the Continental pronunciation)—they generally denote strength, the male sex, affirmation, distance, &c. ; while the same words with the weak or soft vowels, *e, i,* the consonantal skeleton, frame, or groundwork of the word remaining the same — express weakness, the female sex, negation, proximity, and a whole series of corresponding ideas.

" A few examples will demonstrate this. Thus, for instance, the idea of father is expressed in Mantchoo (one of the Ural-Altaic languages) by *ama*, while mother is *eme*. This gives, no doubt, but a very incomplete idea of that peculiarity, but it will perhaps be sufficient to explain in a measure what we found analogous in the Dakota language. Instances of the kind are certainly of rare occurrence in the latter, and we will content ourselves with giving here only a very few examples, in which the above difference of signification is seen to exist, though the significance of the respective vowels seems to be just the reverse, which would in nowise invalidate the truth of the preceding statement, since the same inconsistent alteration or anomaly frequently takes place also in the family of Ural-Altaic languages.

" Thus we find in the Dakota or Sioux language, hɛpaɳ, second son of a family, and hʌpaɳ, second daughter of a family ; ćiɳ, elder brother; ćuɳ, elder sister ; ciɳksi, son ; ćuɳksi, daughter, &c. Also, the demonstratives koɳ, that, and kiɳ, this, the (the definite articles), seem to come, in some respects, under this head.

" To investigate the grammatical structure of languages from a comparative point of view, is, however, but one part of the work of the philologist ; the other equally essential part consists in the study of the words themselves, the very material of which languages are made. We do not as yet intend to touch on the question of Dakota words and their possible affinities, but reserve all that pertains to comparative etymology for some other time

The identity of words in different languages, or simply their affinity, may be either immediately recognised, or rendered evident by a regular process of philological reasoning, especially when such words appear, as it were, disguised, in consequence of certain alterations, due to time and to various vicissitudes, whereby either the original vowels or the consonants, or both, have become changed. Then, also, it frequently happens that one and the same word, when compared in cognate languages, may appear as different parts of speech, so that in one of them it may exist as a noun, and in another only as a verb, &c. Moreover, the same word may have become gradually modified in its original meaning, so that it denotes, for instance, in one of the cognate languages, the *genus*, and in another, merely the *species* of the same thing or idea. Or it may also happen that when several synonymous expressions originally existed in what we may call a mother language, they have become so scattered in their descent, that only one of these words is found in a certain *one* of the derived languages, while others again belong to *other* cognate tongues, or even their dialects, exclusively.

" The foregoing is sufficient to account for the frequent failures in establishing the relationship of certain languages in regard to the affinity of all their *words*. On this occasion it will be enough to mention in passing, as it were, one or two of the most frequently-used words, such as the names of father and mother. In regard to these familiar expressions, we again find a surprising coincidence between the tongues of Upper Asia—or, more extensively viewed, the Ural-Altaic or Tartar-Finnish stock of languages—and the Dakota.

"Father is in Dakota *ate ;* in Turco-Tartar, *ata ;* Mongolian and its branches, *etsä, etsige ;* in the Finnish languages we meet with the forms *attje, atä,* &c.—they all having $at = et$ as their radical syllable.[1]   Now as to mother, it is in the Dakota

---

[1] This also exists in Old German; *ätti* or *etti* being still used in Suabia for father.—C. G. L.

language *ina ;* and in the Asiatic tongues just mentioned it is *ana, aniya, ine, eniye,* &c.

" Again, we find in the Dakota or Sioux language *taṇin,* which means to appear, to be visible, manifest, distinct, clear. Now we have also in all the Tartar dialects *taṇ, tang,* which means first light ; hence dawn of the morning.[1] From it is derived *tani,* which is the stem or radical part of verbs, meaning to render manifest, to make known, to know ; it also appears in the old Tartar verb stems, *tang-(la)* meaning to understand ; and in its mutilated modern (and Western) form, *ang-(la),* without the initial *t,* which has the same signification. We may mention still *mama,* which, in Dakota, denotes the female breast. We might compare it with the Tartar *meme,* which has the same meaning, if we had not also in almost all European languages the word *mamma (mama)* with the very same fundamental signification, the children of very many different nations calling their mothers instinctively, as it were, by that name, *mamma, mama.*[2]

" We may also assert that even in the *foundation* of words we find now and then some slight analogy between certain characteristic endings in the languages of Upper Asia and the Dakota tongue. Thus, for instance, the termination for the *nomen agens,* which in the Dakota language is *sa,* is in Tartar *tsi, si,* and *dchi ;* Mongolian, *tchi,* &c. We also find in Dakota the postposition *ta* (a constituent part of ek*ta, in, at*), which is a locative particle, and corresponds in form to the postpositions *ta* and *da,* and their several varieties and modifications in the greater part of the Ural-Altaic family of languages.

---

[1] *Din* (day) Hindu ; Saxon, *dagian ;* English, *dawn.*—C. G. L.

[2] *e.g., Mamma,* a breast or pap, Latin, having also the meaning of " a child's word for mother." *Ma,* or *mamma,* occurs in seven African languages ; *ma* or *amma* in nine non-Aryan languages of Europe and Asia ; *ama* once in North Australia ; *hammah* in Lewis Murray Island; *mamma* once in Australia ; and *amama* among the Hudson's Bay Esquimaux. *Vide* Sir J. Lubbock's " Origin of Civilisation."—C. G. L.

The same remark applies in a measure to the Dakota postposition *e*, which means to, toward, &c. By means of such postpositions the declension of nouns is effected in the Ural-Altaic languages. The Dakota cases of declension, if we can use this term, amount likewise to a very rude sort of *agglutination*, or rather simple adding of the postpositions to the nouns.[1] There can be here no question of a real inflection or declension, since there is throughout only a kind of loose *adh*esion, and nowhere what we might call a true *co*hesion. The postpositions are in the written language added to the nouns, without being conjoined to them in writing (except the plural ending *pi*), as is also the case in the Mongolian language, the Turco-Tartar dialects, and other tongues of this class.

"In pointing out these various resemblances of the Sioux language to Asiatic tongues we in nowise mean to say that we are inclined to believe in any affinity or remote relationship among them. At this early stage of our researches it would be wholly preposterous to make any assertions as to the question of affinity, &c. All that we intended to do was simply to bring forward a few facts, from which, if they should be further corroborated by a more frequent recurrence of the phenomena here touched upon, the reader might perhaps draw his own conclusions, at least so far as a *very remote* Asiatic origin of the Dakota language is concerned. Further investigations in the same direction might possibly lead to more satisfactory results."

I am confident that few readers will object to the length of this citation, or to its character, since it certainly illustrates forcibly, in several respects, the present condition of all our conjectures, or knowledge, if I may so call it, of the early relations between America and Asia. There is enough in it, as in the narrative of

[1] Declension by means of postpositions also occurs in the Gipsy or Rommany language.—C. G. L.

Hoei-shin, to amply warrant research, and to encourage labour in the direction pointed out; but it would be in the highest degree rash and arrogant to assume, on no better grounds than the two present, that America was settled by the Mongolian race.   Indeed, I cannot too warmly commend Mr Roehrig's extreme caution in advancing his observations.   Nevertheless, I think that they indicate a most decided possibility of an Eastern origin ; and with regard to Hoei-shin, I believe there is good ground for probability.   And in all such cases, one discovery strengthens the other.

CHAPTER XI.

THE MOUND-BUILDERS AND MEXICANS.

THERE is as yet great confusion in our knowledge of the different races of ancient America. For, admitting that the Sioux language, or any North American Indian language, presents traces of Asiatic derivation, this would simply prove that the Sioux came from Asia. But it would not explain the origin of the Aztec race, nor would it cast the least light on the nature of the Mound-Builders, or tell us who or what the people were whom Hoei-shin found, possibly in Mexico. With regard to these early races, some observations by an American writer may not be deemed out of place :[1]—

"Centuries before the Red Indian appeared on the Northern Continent, a race (perhaps of a kindred stock) of higher civilisation dwelt on the western prairies. The 'Mound-Builders,' as they are appropriately called, left their remarkable lines of earthworks from the Lower Mississippi to the Ohio. These structures, on which successive forests of various growths have flourished and died, still survive, and surprise the stranger by their intricacy, skill, and the evidences of vast labour which they display.

[1] New York *Times*.

Some are temples, some burial-places, some are fortifications, some are gardens, some are representations on a gigantic scale of the forms of animals and birds, for what purpose it is difficult to explain. Among these structures are mounds in the form of truncated pyramids, which seem to be the first suggestions of the pyramidal and terraced structures in Central America and Mexico, which, perhaps, formed the highest material works of this mysterious race. They must have conducted an inland commerce over a vast territory, and obtained or purchased mica from the North Carolina mountains, copper from Lake Superior, obsidian from Mexico, specular iron from Missouri, and salt from Michigan—articles which the Red Indians never possessed, except by accident. They understood a rude agriculture, and the arts of weaving and of moulding pottery and figures of animals. They even at times melted copper, and used it in instruments, though they never seem to have done this with iron. The forms of their skulls, and the evidences from their arts, show a milder and more cultivated race than any the whites have ever known north of Central America. Who they were, whence they came, of what blood or stock, is hidden in the mists of a far antiquity. They spread their busy life, and left their traces over the whole Central West, perhaps existing there as long as the Anglo-Saxon race has existed, and then they perished—their only history being written on the ground, a record obliterated by the growth of forests for uncounted centuries, but now partly deciphered by a people of whom they never dreamt. Before even the Mound-Builders, lived a lower and more primeval race, the companions, in all probability, of the fossil animals, a race whose skulls are just being discovered near Chicago, and whose contemporaries have left their stone implements beneath the volcanic deposits of the Sierras. This prehistoric and primeval man belonged to tribes as low and degraded as the present Australians; indeed, of a type more nearly approaching the simian than any hitherto discovered (with the single exception of that of the 'Neanderthal' skull.)"

The extinction of such a vast and widely-spread race as was that of the Mound-Builders, in all probability by the fierce and powerful Red Indian, indicates an immense extent of time. For as by no possibility could any mere migrations from Asia have sufficed to sweep them away, it follows that their exterminators must have long been growing in numbers before they could effectually put an end to them. The writer from whom I have quoted remarks, probably with truth, that the Mound-Builders were a milder and gentler race than their successors, and far more intellectual, as is shown by their skulls. The thoroughness with which this numerous and widely-spread people were exterminated, and the fact that no tradition of them has ever been found among the Red Indians, indicate a very remote age as the period of their disappearance. And yet it is quite certain that if, as Hoei-shin asserts, the mild and highly-refined religion of Buddha ever took root among early Americans, it must have been with such people as the Mound-Builders who practised some vast and dreamy Nature-worship, which would render them peculiarly susceptible to the teachings of the monks. For that they did practise some such religion would appear from this, that since works like theirs were in every other part of the world invariably erected under the influence of belief, it is very unlikely that they formed structures many miles in length, employing probably the labour of millions, for mere amusement. It must have been either among such a race, or by highly-civilised Aztecs, that the monks were welcomed. But it is most unlikely that Buddhism ever made any mark upon the Aztec monarchy itself, or upon the fierce Tolteks. Had it done so, we should find its traces to this day. There is a wonderful leaven in Buddhism ; it penetrates deeply wherever it goes ; it changes strong and energetic faiths ; it even blended intimately with the vigorous Greek element in Northern India.

Meanwhile antiquarians are constantly collecting new facts, which indicate a mysterious knowledge by the Mexicans of many phenomena of the so-called Old World. Even while writing, I learn that Señor José Ostiz de Tapia has now in New York a museum of Mexican antiquities, which is said to be by far the most important ever yet made. This gentleman, who has been for many years investigating the arch· æology of Central America, has collected many thousand objects. One of these is a remarkable stone image, said, according to Indian tradition, to be that of Cucumaz, the God of the Air. " It is cut from a block of chocolate-coloured porphyry, is about two feet high, and about eighteen inches in diameter. The shape is that of a feathered serpent in a solid coil, from whose widely-distended mouth the head of a woman emerges, her arms and legs appearing between the coils. This is supposed to represent the creation of woman. The type of her face bears no likeness to that of any race which ever lived in Mexico, but much resembles

H

the sculptured faces found in Egyptian ruins. Another singular curiosity, that also appears to connect the New with the Old World in prehistoric times, is an image cut from a black stone in the likeness of a negro. Not only are the features of the true Ethiopian type, but the shape of the head and the conformation of the figure. Both these small statues are admirably carved and finished, although their worshippers were certainly ignorant of the use of iron."

So were the ancient Egyptians; but, like the Mexicans, they had copper, which the latter, as it has been proved, brought from Lake Superior; and the Egyptians made bronze as hard as iron, an art but recently rediscovered. Yet all such testimony requires thoroughly scientific treatment. The day has gone by when loose hearsay evidence and wild conjecture passed current for very fair archæology or ethnology. The man who cannot absolutely prove a fact beyond all suspicion of forgery, exaggeration, and chance coincidence, must be satisfied to offer his conjectures very modestly, and merely with the hope that they will attract the attention of others who may deem the hint thus given of sufficient importance to develop by further investigation. Discoveries like those of the Spanish archæologist may be multiplied *ad infinitum.* But they prove nothing beyond an antecedent probability. And as I have kept this strictly in mind through every sentence of this work, having specially selected the illustration by Mr Roehrig on the affinities of the languages in preference to others, on account of its *cautious* spirit, I trust that I may not be accused of positively believing that the " discovery " of America by Buddhist monks is an established fact.

It is, however, more than merely probable that we shall yet make very important discoveries as to the Mound-Builders of America. An immense stock of their remains are still buried, and, in the present rudimentary state of the archæology of prehistoric man, little has been done—very little—with the material which has been gathered. The following brief notice from the *Saturday Review* of a recent work on the subject, sums up in reality nearly all that is known of the mysterious race which once covered such an immense extent of American soil with works strikingly like those of the Old World :—

"No one," says the reviewer, " will long remain in uncertainty whether the Mound-Builders were or were not the ancestors of the tribes who succeeded them in their possession. The author of ' Prehistoric Races ' [1] is in no such perplexity ; nor do we think that any one who compares the two will long remain in uncertainty. The vast size of the mound-works, their enormous number, and their elaborate formation, imply conditions wholly unlike those described in the volume already noticed. They imply not a thin population of free hunters and warriors, obtaining a fairly comfortable but uncertain sustenance by the chase and fishing and a scanty agriculture, but a vast nation,

[1] Prehistoric Races of the United States of America, by Y. W. Foster, LL.D., author of the " Physical Geography of the Mississippi Valley," &c. Chicago : Griggs & Co. ; London : Trübner & Co., 1873.— *Saturday Review*, Aug. 30, 1874.

well fed by the labour of a portion only of its available numbers,
and therefore able to spend immense toil on such constructions;
governed, probably, by powerful princes able to dispose of the
exertions of their people at their pleasure; and, if Dr Foster is
right, an extensive empire under a single rule, able to rely on
the frontier defences for the security of the interior.   We have
lately noticed other works on this subject, and it will therefore
suffice to state in this place that Dr Foster's book is one of the
best and clearest accounts we have seen of those grand monuments of a forgotten race, and to note its peculiar merits.   The
most important of these is the distinct judgment expressed on
the purpose of these works.   They may be divided into three
classes : the animal mounds, or imitations of animal forms, in
rude but gigantic earthworks, chiefly to be found in Wisconsin,
to which it is difficult to assign any object, except one of religion
or commemoration ; those which, square or round in shape,
appear to have been intended as the foundations of temple obser-
vatories for the worship of the heavenly bodies, or of dwellings
(often crowded together in such numbers that we can hardly
assign any but the latter purpose), and yet not entrenched ; and
those works which are distinctly entrenchments, often containing
mounds of the second class.   It is possible, we suppose, that the
mounds of the second class may have been separately stockaded,
and in that case they would have been easily defensible ; but
where several are found near together with no entrenchments
connecting them, it is difficult to think that defence was their
primary purpose.   On the other hand, the earthworks which
enclose great spaces of land generally appear, by their form and
location, to have been fortifications; and Dr Foster observes
that they rarely appear in the centre of the region occupied by
these monuments, but rather on its northern border, where the
empire would be chiefly exposed to the incursions of warlike
enemies.   To the question, what has become of the builders, the
author replies by citing traditions of the earlier and more civilised possessors of Mexico, which indicate that they once occu-

pied a much more northerly settlement, and were driven thence by conquering enemies. The absence of any relics of stone buildings on the mounds, compared with the grand stone ruins of Mexico, forms an obstacle to the identification of the earlier Mexicans with the Mound-Builders; but it is barely possible that a people who built entirely with wood in an alluvial country might learn to erect vast buildings of stone in one of a different character. And a long period may have elapsed between the ejection of the Mound-Builders and the Aztec conquest of Mexico —a period sufficient to account for great changes in the habits of the emigrant race. For we know, at least, that two successive forest growths have covered many of the mounds since they were abandoned, each of which must have occupied centuries, and may have occupied almost any length of time. The Indians appear to have had no tradition of the Mound-Builders, no story of their conquest, no legend even to account for the existence of the mounds. ' Our fathers found them here when they came' is surely not the sole reminiscence of a great war, and of the conquest of a civilised people and a fortified empire, that would linger among the children of the conquerors. Such an answer seems to imply either the interposition of a second race and a second extermination, or an enormous lapse of time, sufficient to extinguish the very memory of such a history as always lingers longest in the minds of a warlike race—a history, too, of which the monuments were always under their eyes."

Assuming these deductions as representing the state of our knowledge of the Mound-Builders, it would seem more probable that they preceded the present inhabitants in Western America by hundreds, or even thousands, of years, than that they were known to the Buddhist priests whom we suppose may have visited their land. It is possible—though it is as yet anything but capable of demonstration—that the civilised races of old New Mexico, as we still see them represented in the Pueblos, were descended from the Mound-Builders, and that their ancestors were exterminated or driven to the south by a rude, fierce, semi-Mongol race, which, derived from Asia, gradually changed its characteristics with climate and intermixture, until it became the present Red Indian. For it is very certain that thousands of American Indians, particularly those of short stature, or of the dwarfish tribes, bear a most extraordinary likeness to Mongols. A closer study of the Indians remaining in New Mexico would throw light on this question. Meanwhile, it may be temporarily assumed that, as nearly every point in Hoei-shin's narrative seems to agree more or less with something known of the Mexican, Peruvian, or New Mexican history or legends, it was not with the old Mound-Builders that the monks came in contact.

CHAPTER XII.

THE reader may recall that in the record of Hoei-shin he speaks particularly of the *images* of Buddha, in connection with the holy writings and religion of that great reformer, as having been taken to America in the year 458 by his five predecessors. I mention this, that in case any other inquirer may investigate this subject, he may pay particular attention to the discovery of such images, or to possible imitations of them, in America, and among its monuments. For to present the sacred likeness of Buddha to the eyes of the world was held to be of itself almost enough to convert unbelievers. To say that these images were made by millions would be no exaggeration. When, in the year 955, the Emperor She-tsung placed severe restrictions on the Buddhist religion, more than 30,000 temples were destroyed, and a mint was established for the purpose of converting such of the images, &c., as were made of precious metals, copper or bronze, into money. Again, in the persecution of 845, "the copper images and bells were melted down and made into cash." It is then probable, that wherever anything could be carried these compactly-formed images were taken.

Professor Neumann speaks of Buddhist emissaries having penetrated to Europe. It is not unlikely, and I am reminded of it by the fact that I was very recently shown a Buddhistic image found in digging for the St Pancras Railway above Midland Yard, about the month of December 1872. It was discovered at a depth of fifteen feet, nine feet of which consisted of loose soil or debris of a recent character, but the remaining six feet were hard, solid earth. The character of the latter, and comparisons with similar excavations, judged by the ages of coins found, indicate a probability that the image may have been left where it was discovered 1000 years ago, or more. I regret that it was impossible for me to obtain this relic for some national museum or other institution, and also that it had been broken, by being ignorantly used as a child's toy, though it was quite perfect when first discovered. The man who dug it up spoke of fragments of similar images having been found; but owing to his ignorance, nothing whatever can be inferred as to whether they were Buddhistic or not.

Images resembling the ordinary Buddha have been found in Mexico and Central America, but they cannot be proved to be identical with it. Their attitude is an extremely natural one for any man not encumbered with tight nether garments to assume in a warm climate; indeed, it is the ordinary sitting position of all men who are not accustomed to chairs. At a grand ball given by the Khedive at Cairo, in 1873, I saw several native gentlemen, after sitting down on chairs, forgetfully draw their feet up under them, and sit in precisely the manner of Buddha.

THE ADVOCATES AND OPPONENTS

OF THE

NARRATIVE OF HOEI-SHIN.

DEGUIGNES, KLAPROTH, AND D'EICHTHAL.

CHAPTER XIII.

DEGUIGNES, KLAPROTH, AND D'EICHTHAL.

THE reader has probably inferred, from the allusions to Deguignes in Professor Neumann's work, that the Chinese discovery of Fusang is no novelty to the world of science. More than a century ago that sagacious and sensible *savant* discussed in the " Mémoires de l'Académie des Inscriptions et Belles Lettres" (vol. xxviii., 1761), " Les Navigations des Chinois du côté de l'Amérique, et sur plusieurs Peuples situés à l'extrémité de l'Asie Orientale," and endeavoured to confirm the memoir by Hoei-shin. The Chinese scholar Klaproth attempted to refute Deguignes, but employed arguments which a more recent writer, D'Eichthal, with the aid of far more extended and accurate information, has in turn refuted. It is true, Deguignes was no more able to absolutely *prove* that Hoei-shin and his predecessors were in California, than we are at the present day. But he did his best, by adducing such testimony as he could collect; and we have at least the satisfaction of knowing that something has been added to it, and that more may be contributed, until at last the work shall be completed.

A thorough history of the question would have made it proper to begin with Deguignes, or rather with Kampfer (bk. i. c. iv.), who speaks so positively of the great Eastern Continent beyond Kamtschatka, discovered by the Japanese. But as the translation by Neumann from the Chinese original is more complete, and as he has succinctly set forth the whole question as it was in his time, I judged it best to give preference to the translation of his work, and then add the letter of Colonel Kennon, which refers directly to so many statements made by Neumann— a course which will not seem out of place to those who will bear in mind that Colonel Kennon, who has accurately surveyed and mapped every mile of the North Pacific, and every acre of its shores on either side, is therefore as practically familiar with the possibilities of the route as any man can be. The importance of his testimony at the present day, and the advanced state of our geographical knowledge, will appear to those who will consult the curious Japanese map brought to Europe by Kampfer, and given by him to Hans Sloane, representing the North Pacific ; or the almost as erroneous chart of the same by Philippe Buache, which is given with a facsimile of the former in Deguignes' Memoir ("Memoires de Lit. et de l'Académie Royale des Inscriptions et Belles Lettres," vol. xxviii., 1761). Having done this, I propose

to present in a condensed form an examination of the
whole subject as it appeared in 1864 to M. Gustave
d'Eichthal, a scholar well known for his learning and
enthusiasm in Greek literature and other subjects.
But before passing to the work of M. G. d'Eichthal, I
shall touch on a few points in the excellent article
by Deguignes, which should not be neglected.   He
himself regarded the facts which he had collected
as authentic, and not as mere conjectures, like those
indulged in by Grotius, Deläet, and others, relative to the early settlement of America—of which
latter I may observe, that the reader who is desirous to know what they are, can find them all
appropriately set forth and commented on in Irving's
" Knickerbocker History of New York," a most fitting
receptacle for theories which by their absurdity have
become the legitimate property of the humorist.
Deguignes attempted honestly and modestly to adhere
to observation and probability, and the result is that
his ideas have been, in part at least, confirmed, and the
arguments of his opponents proved unsound.

His first step was to show that Li-yen, a Chinese
historian who lived at the beginning of the seventh
century, speaks of a country named Fou-sang (Fusang)
which was more than 40,000 *li* east of the eastern shore
of China.   To reach it, " one must depart from the
province of Lean-tong, north of Pekin, and that after
travelling 12,000 *li*, the traveller would reach Japan ;
and thence to the north, after a journey of 7000 *li*,

arrive at the country of Ven-chin " (Wen-schin, the Painted People). " Five thousand *li* from this country, towards the east, is Ta-han, which is 20,000 *li* from Fou-sang." As Deguignes remarked, " Of all these, we only know the Leao-tong, the northern province of China, whence vessels sailed; and Japan, which was the principal station for Chinese vessels. The three other points on the journey are the Ven-chin country, Ta-han, and Fou-sang. I hope to show that the first is Jeso, the second Kamtschatka, and the third a place about California."

The next step was naturally enough to determine what was the length of a *li* in China in the fifth century. But this was difficult ; for, as Deguignes remarks, " Although at the present day 250 *li* make a degree, they have varied in the past, not only under different dynasties, but in different provinces. Father Gaubil, who made deep researches in Chinese astronomy, did not venture to decide this measure. He tells us that the greater portion of the *literati* under the reign of Han maintained that a thousand *li*, drawn from south to north, made a difference of an inch of shadow at noon on a dial of eight feet. Those who succeeded them thought that this measurement was incorrect, since they judged according to the standard of the *li* in vogue in their own time. But if we cast our eyes on the *li* adopted by the astronomers of the dynasty of Leam, who flourished at the beginning of the sixth century (" Observations Astronomiques du Pére Gaubil," vol. ii.), we shall find a considerable difference, since their 250 *li* from north to south give in like manner an inch in difference. . . . . But uncertainty may in this case be avoided by observing that from Leao-tong to the island of Toni-ma-tao is fixed as a distance of 7000 *li*, and, in accordance with the *li* thus established, the 12,000 *li* from Leao-tong to Japan end in the centre of the island, about Mea-co, its capital."

Deguignes determined, with great intelligence, that the country of the Wen-schin, 7000 *li* north-west of Japan, must be Jeso, from the exact agreement of the accounts given of that country by Chinese historians of the early part of the sixth century (Goei-chi and Ven-hien-tum-hao, A.D. 510–515) with that of Dutch navigators in 1643 ("Ambassade des Hollandois au Japon," vol. i. p. 10; "Recueil des Voyages au Nord," vol. iii. p. 44). Both describe the extraordinary appearance of the natives, and speak of the abundance of a peculiar mineral resembling quicksilver. "Five thousand *li* from this country, to the east, lies Tahan. The manners of the people here were like those of Wen-schin, but they spoke a different language."

I trust that it will be specially observed by those who think the journey from China to Aliaska improbable, on account of the dreariness of the country and its great discomfort, that the old travellers cited by Deguignes speak of the Chinese navigators as habitually passing through many Tartar tribes, crossing the Great Desert of Chamo, passing over the ice of a great lake in the country of Ko-li-han, and, north of it, through a chain of mountains, where the nights in summer were so short that one could hardly roast a leg (or breast) of mutton between sunset and sunrise. But the degree to which the dreariness of a country will deter a traveller must depend upon the traveller himself. Colonel Kennon, in his letter, speaks of the years which he passed in a little pilot-boat, on probably the very route traversed by Hoei-shin, as the happiest of his life; while, as to the land, Lieutenant Cochran, who in 1823 had the hardihood to go on foot from St Petersburg to Kamtschatka, found the latter country delightful, and speaks with pleasure of the entertainments there. It is true that he there wooed and won a wife, an incident of all others most likely to convey sunshine into what all writers agree is the foggiest country in the world. It is, however, to be assumed, that Hoei-shin and his predecessors went by sea —no impossible thing, at a time when in China both astronomy and navigation were sciences in a high sense of the word. Deguignes, speaking of the winds and currents, as Colonel Kennon does, says that the Chinese, in order to avoid the shores, "took the wind from the north of Japan, and in the Sea of Jeso sailed to the east; but at the Strait of Uriés the current bore them rapidly to the north." Therefore they entered the Strait of Uriés, beyond which they found *many islands*, which extend to the most northern point of Kamtschatka,

and where also terminate the 5000 *li* between Jeso and
Tahan. The account of the different people inhabiting
the North of Asia on the route to America, as given
by Deguignes from several old Chinese historians, is
far more detailed than that in Neumann. From this
and other circumstances, I infer that Professor Neumann,
though he cites Deguignes, had read his work with but
little care. Deguignes apologises for his long and
detailed account of these tribes, their manner of life
and habits ; but to the interested reader this will appear
to be one of the strongest links in the chain of evidence,
since no one on perusing it can doubt that the Chinese
were perfectly familiar with the entire northern country
to the very edge of America, and had been so for many
generations. Deguignes does not appear to have re-
flected that the *naïf* and manifestly truthful accounts of
all these different tribes by old historians strengthen
his arguments, since he tells us that he has omitted
most of them. It is worth noting that he cites from
Ven-hien-tum-kao and Tam-chu that " the Chinese
travellers who intended to visit Tahan took their departure from a city north of the river Hoam-ho,[1] towards
the country of the Ortous [2] Tartars. This town, then
called by the Chinese *Tchung-cheou-kiang-tching*, must
be the one now known as Piljo-tai-hotun." This mention of the route as that which was usually followed
indicates that there was in those days much travel in
that direction ; and we find a reason for it when we

[1] Hoang-hoin.   [2] Ordos or Hotas.

learn that at an earlier period the chain of islands from
Asia to America was incredibly rich in furs, and that
at a time when furs were in extraordinary demand in
Europe and the East, a demand which lasted until the
fifteenth century.   We are told, for instance, that the
principal charge brought against a Turkish sultan of that
time, when his subjects rose in rebellion, was that he had
spent millions in purchasing sables, this fur being supposed to be possessed of virtues as an aphrodisiac.   To
secure this luxury any sum was given ; and it is said that,
so far back as the fifth century, the Che-goei tribes, who
lived on the north banks of the Amur, were principally
occupied in fishing and in hunting sables.   This fur-hunt-
ing extended over the Aleutian Islands, which, as D'Eichthal remarks (*Revue Archæologique*, 1862, vol. ii. p. 197),
were inhabited before their conquest by the Russians
(1760–1790) by a numerous and prosperous population.
" As we leave the North," says Maury (*Revue des Deux
Mondes*, April 1858), " the facilities of crossing by short
voyages increase, and the natives seem to find more and
more attraction in them.   With nothing but a leafy
branch for a sail, the boat-load, consisting generally of
a man, his wife and children, dashes out seawards as
soon as a favourable wind blows, and proceeds at a fast
rate."   The Russians have long had establishments
on the islands of St Paul and St George, whence they
send vast quantities of furs ; and Colonel Kennon
has frequently, while conversing with me, spoken of the
beautiful quality of many which he saw, but which he

was unable either to purchase or accept as a gift, owing to a special request from the Russian Government that he would not take one away. Whatever he needed for food or stores was supplied with great generosity, but no furs could be touched. I have called special attention to the furs of this region, since, as they were once much more abundant there than at present, and that at a time when it was more the fashion to wear them, we have a satisfactory reason to account for the Chinese having at one time been familiar with the island route to America, and for their having gradually abandoned it. I am not aware that any special stress has been laid on this as evidence, but to my mind it fully accounts for the tone of the old writers cited by Deguignes, who appear to speak of going to America, not as if it were a legendary exploit, which had once or twice been achieved in the early dawn of history, but rather as a common incident.

Tam-chu states that it is fifteen days' travel from the Che-goei, or sable-hunters of the Northern Amur to the east, where are found the Yu-tche, a race derived from the Che-goei; and that a further journey of fifteen days brought the traveller to Tahan. But, he adds, people also reached Tahan by sea, sailing from Jeso. After careful examination, Deguignes determined that the only country 20,000 *li* east of China, to which the name and conditions of Fusang could possibly be applicable, must be California or New Mexico.

" The Chinese historians add to the account of Hoei-shin that of a Kingdom of Women, which is 1000 *li* farther east." It has been ingeniously suggested by M. D'Eichthal, that as the term *women* was formerly applied to entire tribes in North America, the monk may have heard something of them. Thus the Delawares, having given up their arms to the Six Nations, and become *protégés* of the latter, were formally entitled women, and accepted the name at a grand congress of the tribes. As for the absurdities connected with this legend of the women, as given by Hoei-shin, it is sufficient to say that he uses the term "it is said" in reference to the statement that the children of this woman-realm appear matured at the age of three years. Had he pretended to have visited the country, he would not have given as a matter of hearsay what he must certainly have observed. And as he was also told that these women suckled their babes from the backs of their heads, Deguignes, with his usual sagacity, remarks, " It is easy to see by this narrative that the women fed their children *par dessus leurs épaules*— over their shoulders—as is done in many places in India." The following, from the historians Nan-su and Ven-hien-tum-kao, is not without interest, as showing that from an early age Chinese vessels were driven by storms to America :—" In the year 507 (A.D.), under the dynasty of Leam, a Chinese vessel sailing in these seas was blown by a tempest on an unknown island. The women resembled those of China, but the men had faces and voices like dogs. These people ate small beans, wore dresses made of a kind of cloth, and the walls of their houses were built of earth, raised in a circle. The Chinese could not understand them." If we make allowance for the dogs' faces on the well-known ground that the Chinese are particularly given to applying the word *dog* to all people whom they regard as savages, it will be found that the description applies with marvellous exactness to those New Mexican Indians who held a middle place between such highly-cultivated people as the Pueblos and the wilder and ruder tribes. The resemblance of the women to those of China is a matter of common remark; and one of my own earliest observations, as a boy, was the extraordinary likeness of Afong-Moy, a Chinese woman who visited America many years ago, to an ordinary squaw. This likeness is always, however, more striking in half-breed Indian women, and in those of light complexion, and the Pueblos are very much lighter than other Indians.[1] The enormous consumption of beans (*frijoles*), the cloth (which was very beautifully made by the Pueblo-Aztecs, from early ages), and especially the circular walls of earth, all identify these Indians with those of New Mexico.[2] These people, as well as the Indians of Louisiana (Chevalier de Tonti,

[1] Captain H. C. Leonard, who has resided for twenty-five years among the Chinooks, and who is familiar with all the North-western tribes, fully confirms this statement relative to the general resemblance of their squaws to Chinese women.

[2] For an account of their dwellings, *vide* Johnson's "Cyclopædia," N.Y., 1874.

" Voyage au Nord "), had a curious habit of howling and roaring terribly to express respect and admiration, and this may account for the voices like dogs spoken of by the Chinese.

Deguignes has collected some curious instances from old writers which seem to prove that Chinese merchants frequently found their way to Western America. Thus George Horne[1] (l. 6, c. 5), relates that beyond the tribes which dwelt west of the Hurons, there came in great vessels strangers who were beardless. Fr. Vasquez de Coronado states that he found at Quivir vessels with gilded poops; and Pedro Melendez, in Acosta, speaks of the wrecks of Chinese vessels seen on the coast. " And it is beyond question that foreign merchants, clothed in silk, formerly came among the Catacualcans." All these reports intimate that the Chinese once traded in Northern California, about the country of the Quivir. And there is, moreover, ground for asserting that, at one time certainly, the most civilised tribes in North America were those nearest China. It is generally assumed that the intelligent and almost refined Pueblos of New Mexico are the descendants of Aztecs who fled to the north after the Spanish invasion; but the traditions of the Aztecs themselves declare that they came from the north, and it is probable that the Pueblos have always been where they are. Delaët (bk. vi. c. xvi. and xxii.) says that near New Mexico were people who dwell in houses

---

[1] *Vide* Delaët, bk. vi.

several stories high, with halls, chambers, and stoves. They wore skins and cotton cloths, but, what is unusual among savages, had leather shoes and boots. Every district had its public criers, who announced the king's orders, and idols and temples were everywhere. Baron de la Hontan ("Memoires sur l'Amerique") speaks of the Mirambecs, who inhabited walled towns near a *great Salt Lake.* These people made cloths, copper hatchets, and other wares.

Charlevoix ("Histoire de la Nouvelle France") narrates two incidents, which, though almost incredible, are at least worthy of consideration. One of these is that Father Grellon, after acting as missionary for some time in Canada, went to China, and thence to Tartary, where he met a Huron woman whom he had formerly known in Eastern America. Another Jesuit, returning from China, also declared that a Spanish woman, originally of Florida, was found by him in Tartary, to which country she had come by an extremely cold northern route.

It is said that the walrus and seal hunters of the mouth of the river Kocoima, in Siberia, are often carried out to sea on vast floating fields of ice, and occasionally drift to the opposite American shore, which is not far distant. Most of my readers will recall the wonderful preservation of the crew of the *Polaris,* which, with women and children, drifted for many months on an ice-cake. Indeed, many wild animals, also like men engaged in hunting, may in this way have been transported from one continent to the other.

These are substantially the points advanced by De-guignes,[1] an excellent Chinese scholar, and a careful writer. It was while making researches for a history of the Mongols that he found in the works of old Chinese historians the materials for his theory that America was peopled from the North-west. In 1831 Julius Heinrich von Klaproth, a distinguished scholar, attacked Deguignes in a work entitled " Recherches sur le Pays de Fou-sang mentionné dans les Livres Chinois, et pris mal à propos pour une partie de l'Amérique " (" Nouvelles Annales des Voyages," t. xxi. de la deuxième série, 1831). By this work, according to Gustave d'Eichthal, Klaproth did much harm. There was an authority attached to his name which made it easy for him to render ridiculous the ideas advanced by Deguignes. There is a popular tendency—especially in France—to ridicule everything Chinese; and in England the mere idea of Chinese metaphysics awakens a smile in the readers of Dickens, though scholars know that Chinese Buddhists may be fairly said to have exhausted every refinement of thought known to *à priori* or pantheistic methods. In ninty-nine cases out of a hundred, the sneering critic who negatives has it all his own way with the public for a time, and for more than the present time he does not care. The

[1] Histoire Générale des Huns, des Turcs, des Mongoles, et des autres Tartares Occidentaux, Paris, 1756–58, 4 vols., par Joseph Deguignes.

refutation of Klaproth now appears worthless; he produces nothing new, and attacks Deguignes entirely " out of himself." He begins with a plausible quibble, by accusing Deguignes of being false to his title. " In the Chinese original," says Klaproth, " which Deguignes had before his eyes, there is nothing said of the navigation undertaken by the Chinese to the land of Fusang; but, as may be seen further on, it turns upon a notice of Fusang as given by a Buddhist priest who had been there." Klaproth says " a native of the country," and by the country he means Fusang. But in a German version of the same passage, given by Neumann in a more recent work (" Ost-Asien und West-America, Zeitschrift für allgemeine Erdkunde," April 1864), the (or this) country refers to China. Now Deguignes really wrote, according to his title, on the navigation or voyages of Chinese to America, and he says very little of the record of Hoei-shin, beyond quoting it. Deguignes tells us nothing of a Chinese original in his title, he only adduces the narrative as confirming his other researches; and Klaproth appears fully convicted of a shrewd, unscrupulous trick, such as a petty Bohemian might have recourse to in some notorious journal, whose ideal of criticism is to make a writer appear personally ridiculous. After this he makes a vigorous attack on Deguignes' estimate of the length of the Chinese *li* in the fifth century, which ends in nothing, since he thinks that the Chinese of that time had no means of estimating distances at

sea. The remark is that of a man accustomed to
believe that distances cannot be measured at sea without all the appliances and training of modern science,
while the truth is, every captain of a Yankee coaster
knows that it can be done—not very accurately, it is true,
but approximatively or tolerably well—with the simplest
instruments, such as any sailor can make. But as D'Eichthal observes, the 20,000 *li* from Tahan to Fusang are
probably merely arbitrary. The travellers found that,
going at the same average rate, it took them more than
twice as long to get from Tahan to Fusang as from
Leao-tong (north of Pekin) to Tahan. The obvious and
natural way to measure Hoei-shin's 20,000 *li* from
Tahan to Fusang is by the *li* assigned to the preceding
distances, and according to this standard the estimate
is accurate enough.

"The two agree in placing Wen-schin in the island
of Jeso, situated 7000 *li* from the point of departure on
the coast of Niphon. There, in fact, is the country of
the Wen-shin or Tattooed People. The Ainos, who
then occupied the northern part of Japan, or the island
of Jeso, are still accustomed to paint their bodies and
faces with different figures. But here," continues
D'Eichthal, " all agreement between the two writers
ceases. Deguignes thinks that Tahan, which is, according to the Chinese account, 5000 *li* from Jeso, must
be Kamtschatka. In this conclusion he has against
him, it is true, the important sum-total of the distance;
but on the other hand there are many arguments in his

favour, which we shall proceed to examine. Klaproth holds, however, that Tahan is simply the island of Krafto or Taraï-kaï, the southern point of which is found, according to his calculation, exactly 5000 *li* from the northern point of Niphon. To arrive at this conclusion, as the distance is only six degrees, Klaproth is compelled to adopt the measurement of 850 *li* to a degree, which he had just before rejected." He had said that the distance between the West Coast of Corea, and the middle of Niphon is, according to Deguignes, too great. "It would suppose for the *li* a length of 850 to the degree, whereas, at the highest, it cannot be more than 400."

"But to continue. If the island of Taraï-kaï is Tahan, we cannot find Fusang 20,000 *li* to the east, for the nearest land in this direction is 90° distant. ' By taking the story literally,' says Klaproth, ' and by seeking Fusang east of Tahan, we fall into the Pacific Ocean.' " But as Fusang must be found somewhere, and as it was a foregone conclusion with Klaproth that it must not be found in America, he assumes that, having arrived at the southern point of Taraï-kaï, one should sail first to the east in order to pass the Strait of La Pérouse, coasting along the northern shore of Jeso, but that, having arrived at the north-east point of the same island, he would sail to the south, and thus arrive at some part of the South-east Coast of Japan, where Fusang would be found.

It will probably occur to the reader that this would

be taking a deal of pains to destroy an adversary's argument, and weaving a very tangled web. Yet as the last word always has weight, this argument of Klaproth held its own for many years, and still holds it with many people. It is true, as D'Eichthal remarks, that by proceeding in this style Klaproth put himself, in the most arbitrary manner, in direct opposition to the very letter of his text, which says nothing at all about sailing up and down and coasting around islands. " But this is not the only objection which can be urged against him. In the first place, nobody in Japan ever heard of Fusang. The details given with regard to it do not suit Japan in the least. One circumstance is decisive. Not only does the narrator put Fusang 20,000 *li* east of Tahan, but he speaks of a country of women 1000 *li* from Fusang. But 1000 *li* to the east of Japan must be in the sea." It is to be regretted that Klaproth asserts that Fusang is an ancient name of Japan, but without citing any authority on which to support such a serious and very material statement. His arguments have been answered not only by D'Eichthal, but by Sr. José Perez, in an article in the *Révue Orientale et Américaine*, No. 4, pp. 189–195. For a Chinese, even in the sixth century, to place in Japan such a marvellous country as Fusang was popularly supposed to be, would have been quite as absurd as if a French traveller of the fourteenth century had assured the world that he had found in England an immense region inhabited by giants. For popular belief very soon clothed Fusang with incredible marvels, as we shall see anon; and Klaproth supposes this possible of a country which was at the time constantly exchanging embassies with China, and conveying to the latter, as the reader may recall from Neumann's work, detailed accounts of all its provinces, and of their inhabitants. As Klaproth admits, Fusang soon became a fairy-land, which Chinese poets loved to adorn with the fantastic and marvellous. "The authors of Chan-haï-king, of the Li-sao, Hoai-nan-tsu, Li-pe-tai, and others, have found in it an inexhaustible resource. According to them, the sun rises in the valley of Yang-kon and makes his toilet in Fu-sang, where there are mulberry-trees many thousand rods high. The natives eat the fruit, which makes their bodies shine like gold, and confers on them the ability to fly. "Such fables are not placed in a neighbouring country. They require for plausibility great distance, and entirely strange circumstances."

Again, the narrative declares that Buddhism was introduced into Fusang A.D. 458, but it did not find its way into Japan, officially at least, until 552. How then could Fusang, admitting that it existed, have been a part of Japan?

"But to throw full light on the question," says D'Eichthal, "we should study the second itinerary, that by land from China to Tahan, given by Deguignes and Klaproth. We shall now do so; and if accused of delaying too long over these documents, we reply that in them we find, as Deguignes and Klaproth himself had clearly seen, a leading element in the question, and a decisive argument from the geographical point of view for the existence or non-existence of ancient communications between Asia and America.

" The traveller by land from China to Tahan went from the upper course of the Hoang-hoin, in the north of China, passed through the country of the Ordos or Ho-tas, traversed the desert of Cobi, and arrived at the principal camp of the Hoeï-khé Turks, on the left bank of the Orchon, not far from its source, where Kara-korum was afterwards placed.   Thence he journeyed to Lake Baïkal, crossed the country of Ko-li-han, the ancient home of the Kirkis or Khirghiz, and turning to the east, came to the Chy-weï.   The most southern of these lived near the river Onon, flowing from the right of the Upper Amoor (Amur). By travelling fifteen days to the east, or in the direction of the Amoor, were found the Chy-weï Youtché, pro-bably the same people whom other Chinese authors call Youtchy, that is to say, the Djourdje, the ancestors of the present Mongols.   From this point, finally, ten days' journey to the north brought the traveller to Tahan surrounded on three sides by the sea, and also called Lieu-koueï.[1]

" We should have under our eyes the work of Degui-gnes, to realise with what care he has discussed every part of this journey.   Then, having reached the final point, he reasonably remarks, that as one travels by

[1] Klaproth, pp. 62, 64 ; Deguignes, pp. 508–510.

land all the way to arrive at Tahan, it cannot be an island, yet that it must be a maritime country according to the first route, since they also went thither by sea; and basing his statement on the two views, he places the *point de recontre* of the two itineraries in Kamtschatka."

"The southern part of Kamtschatka, or Tahan," says Deguignes, "was known to the Chinese under the name of Lieou-koueï. Of old, the Tartars who lived near the river Amoor reached it after fifteen days' sailing to the north (Deguignes traces this navigation on his map). Chinese historians relate that this country is surrounded by the sea on three sides. In the year 640 (A.D.), the King of Lieou-koueï sent his son to China.[1] According to the most accurate descriptions which the Russians have given of it, this country is a tongue of land extending from north to south, from Cape Sultoï-noss to the north of Jeso, with which many writers have confounded it. It is partly separated from the rest of Siberia by a gulf of the Eastern Sea, which passes from south to north. Towards the northern ex-

[1] These details regarding Kamtschatka are reproduced in an article by Professor Neumann, "Ost-Asien und West-America, Zeitschrift für allgemeine Erdkunde" (April 1864). Professor Neumann, says D'Eichthal, gives his citations as from Steller's "Beschreibung von dem Laude Kamtschatka" (Leipzig, 1830), but they were originally drawn from Chinese works. In Neumann's statement, the envoy of the son of the king of Lieou-koueï, in China, is mentioned in this manner—"In the year 640 of our era, in the time of the second Emperor of Tang, the Empire of the South received the last embassy and the last tribute from the country of Lieou-koueï" (p. 316). I have throughout used Deguignes' original work in verification of D'Eichthal's articles.—C. G. L.

K

tremity it is inhabited by very ferocious people.   Those
who live towards the south are more civilised.   It is
very likely that their commerce with the Japanese and
Chinese merchants who traded on their shores has contributed to make them milder and more sociable than
those of the north, among whom these two more refined
races rarely come " (p. 511).

It is only after discussing the two routes, and
settling the common point or limit as we have seen,
that Deguignes undertakes to determine the position of
the country of Fusang.   " This long detail," he declares,
" was necessary for an exact knowledge of the situation
of the country.   The Chinese narrative informs us that
Fusang is 20,000 *li* distant from Tahan or Kamtschatka.   Thus, by leaving a port in the latter country, such as Avatcha, and sailing *east* for 20,000 *li*, the
voyage ends on the most western shore of America, or
about the place where the Russians landed in 1741.   In
all this immense extent of ocean there is no land nor
island to which the distance of 20,000 *li* applies.   Nor
can we, on the other hand, suppose that the Chinese
followed the coast of Asia, and, touching its most
eastern extremity, there placed the land of Fusang.
The excessive cold which prevails in the north of
Kamtschatka, renders this supposition untenable." [1]

" When Deguignes wrote," adds D'Eichthal, " the

[1] Both Klaproth and Bretschneider have left out of sight the fact that
Fusang as described must have been a temperate, if not a warm climate.
—C. G. L.

solution which he proposed was not, however, so simple
or evident as it may appear to us to-day. At that
time the geography of the North Pacific was just beginning to be cleared of the darkness in which it had been
so long enveloped. Behring had discovered, in 1728,
the strait which bears his name; he had found, in 1741,
some of the Aleutian Isles, the promontory of Aliaska,
and the northern extremity of the American side; but
he had not been able to make exact surveys. Deguignes, at least, did not possess them; and to prepare the
singular map, designed by Philip Buache, which ac-
companies his memoir, the illustrious academician had
recourse to a Japanese chart.

"Since M. De l'Isle," he says, "published a map of
this part of the world, we have obtained from Russia
information which, without giving with accuracy the
contour of the American coasts, teaches us generally that
the coast of California runs towards the west, and
approaches considerably that of Asia, leaving between
the continents a narrow strait, agreeing with the shape
which the first geographers gave to America, probably
from more exact knowledge than we suppose, and which
is now lost." Thus the map of Asia, published by
Sanson in 1650, gives, between Asia and America, near
the place of Behring's Straits, the Strait of Ainan, as
it was then called. This strait disappeared on Guillaume de l'Isle's map of 1723, but reappeared in the
same map re-edited in 1745, and again in 1762, corrected by new documents. This information was con-

firmed by Japanese charts, especially by one which Mr
Hans Sloane, President of the Royal Society of London,
had communicated to him, and which he placed before
his paper in the " Memoires de l'Académie des Inscriptions et Belles-Lettres." " It agrees on the whole," he
declares, " with our old maps of America, and with the
Russian discoveries." " On this map, about the part
discovered by the Russians, America seems to advance
considerably, and form a tongue of land which extends
to Asia (the promontory of Aliaska). *In this case it is
intelligible that the Chinese found it much easier to reach
Fusang, since they thus had a coast to follow almost all
the way.*"

"It was," says M. D'Eichthal very truly, "with a
kind of prophetic instinct, or, if you will, with extreme
shrewdness and sense, that Deguignes traced, on the
map made by him, the route which was probably followed
by those whom he calls *navigateurs chinois* to get to
America.   The details are naturally very imperfect, and
Behring's Island is the only one given of the Aleutians.
On the other hand, the promontory of Aliaska is out of
all proportion too great, both in length and breadth.
There is an entire absence of all astronomical verification ; nevertheless, the general 'lay of the land' is
correct, as recent discoveries have confirmed.   We have
under our eyes three very important documents, 'Les Renseignements Statistiques et Ethnographiques sur les
Possessions Russes à la côté Nord-ouest de l'Amérique,
by Rear-Admiral Wrangel ('Statistical and Ethno-

graphical Communications as to the Russian Possessions on the North-west Coast of America);[1] an analysis
of the work of Father Wenjaminow on ' Les Isles (Aléou-
tiennes) du District du Unalaska,' by F. Löwe (from
the periodical *Archiv für die wissenschaftliche Kunde
von Russland*, 1842, 8th Part) ; and the critique of a
memoir by Maury, on the facilities of passing from the
North-east Coast of Asia to the North-west Coast of
America (*Revue des Deux Mondes*, April 1858). All
of these works agree in demonstrating the ease of this
communication, and that of settling on the North-west
Coast of America. The climate of all this region, even
at the 60th degree of latitude is, for its elevation, very
mild. The chain of the Aleutian Isles and the promontory of Aliaska form, as it were, a barrier which
exclude Polar influences. On the other hand, the
great warm current of the Pacific Ocean, observed by
modern navigators,[2] contributes to raise the temperature.
Observations, carefully collected, have shown that at
Sitka the average temperature is 7°.39 Centigrade, or
5°.91 Reaumur, with, it is true, slight differences between
summer and winter : even in winter the sea is never
closed. In a word, according to the unanimous testimony of navigators, there is not on the face of the

[1] In the original edition, "Statistische und Ethnographische Nachrichten,
gesammelt von Contre-Admiral von Wrangel," St Petersburg, 1839. This
is the first part of the collection called "Beiträge zur Kentniss des Rus-
sischen Reichs, &c., herausgegeben von K. E. von Baer und von Hel-
mersen."—C. G. L.

[2] *Vide* Letter from Colonel Barclay Kennon.

globe such a change of climate as is experienced in passing from Behring's Straits to the Pacific Ocean."

All that has been said of the extreme facility with which the natives of the North Pacific pass from Asia to America has, however, according to M. D'Eichthal, nothing to do with the question of Chinese or Japanese navigation between the continents ; and therefore, he thinks that here Deguignes erred, and said too much, when he entitled his memoir " Des Navigations des Chinois du côté de l'Amérique." It seems to me that this is stretching courtesy to Klaproth to affectation. Deguignes believed, from several sources, that Chinese, merchants as well as missionaries, had found their way to California. On this hypothesis he wrote his book, and demonstrated the route which they must have followed, and therefore he had a full right to say that its subject was on the " navigations " of the Chinese from the American coast. He could not, unfortunately, give the log-books and diaries of the skippers who took Hoei-shin and his predecessors across ; though, if he had, Klaproths would not have been wanting to impugn their authenticity.

It will be remembered that Deguignes lays stress on the high culture of the early dwellers in New Mexico. So far as the limited information of his time extended, he found in that country the point of departure and the first theatre of American civilisation, and he believed, according to D'Acosta, that, instead of the inhabitants of this region having been refugees from Mexico, they are

the remains of a primitive civilisation from which the
Mexicans drew their culture ere they wandered south.
D'Eichthal appeals to ancient works not known to
Deguignes, and also to the most recent, as verifying
this theory. These are the " Narrative of the Journey
of Cibola in 1540," by Castañeda de Nagera, Paris,
1838, given in the collection of " Voyages, Relations,
et Mémoires Originaux, pour servir à l'Histoire de la
Découverte de l'Amérique, par Ternaux Compans ; "
the " Reports of Explorations and Surveys to ascertain
the most practicable and economical route for a railroad
from the Mississippi River, made under the direction
of the Secretary of War in 1853–54," especially in vol.
iii. ; " Report on the Indian Tribes," by Lieutenant A.
W. Whipple, Thomas Ewbank, Esq., and Prof. W. W.
Turner; and also the " Personal Narrative of Explorations, &c.," by John Russell Bartlett, New York, 1854.
In these works may be found, not only indubitable
proof of the former highly-advanced civilisation of New
Mexico, but remarkable indications of apparent affinity
with Chinese culture. Deguignes was in the right
when he suggested that the oxen seen by Hoei-shin
were probably bison. We might add the statement,
that in Fusang stags were raised as cattle are in
China, and that cheese was made from hind's milk,
" as appears from Popol-Vuh, the Sacred Book of the
Quichés," by M. l'Abbé Brasseur de Bourbourg [1] (In-

---

[1] B. de Bourbourg is a writer who must be cited with great caution,
but he is probably right in this instance.—C. G. L.

troduction, p. 40). He was also strictly right in asserting that the vine was known there, and that iron was
not, but that copper was used, and that gold and silver
(owing, doubtless, to their abundance) were of no
value. All these facts were strictly applicable to
Mexico, and they were not collectively applicable to
any country then known to the Chinese. Of his own
knowledge Hoei-shin relates no marvels ; what he tells
us of the existence of a white race is fully confirmed by
tradition and the traces still existing of such people.
Lieutenant Whipple says there are white Indians at
Zuni, the principality of the old kingdom of Cibola,
although they are exceptions. They have, he says, light
or auburn hair. The first Indian seen by Father Niça,
in 1539, is described as a man of light complexion.
Indians of this type have since existed. And Catlin
remarks that, on seeing the Mandans, one is tempted
to exclaim, "These are no Indians." There are numbers of them whose colour is as light as that of half-
breeds, and among the women " are many who are almost
white, and who have grey eyes, or blue and hazel "
(Catlin, " Letters and Notes on the Manners, Customs,
and Conditions of the North American Indians," fourth
edition, London, 1844, vol. i. p. 93). And as some
uncertainty may exist as to the relative colour of a
half-breed, I would explain that it is often not darker
than that of a Chinese, and is much clearer, the cheeks
being generally rosy. I have seen the whole of Catlin's portraits of Mandans, and, like all Americans

who have been in the West, am familiar with Indians, both of full and mixed blood, and am quite sure that such an expert as General Whipple, whom I have known personally very well, never mistook a half-breed for a real Indian. The extraordinary lightness of the Mandan women is a phenomenon which can only be accounted for by their belonging to an entirely different stock from the other tribes. The men had very long hair; braves who were 6 feet 2 inches high had it trailing for two or three inches on the ground.

All these facts agree very well with the assertions of Hoei-shin, and M. D'Eichthal, with great sagacity, points out that even the two prisons, situated one in the north, the other in the south; the one for great criminals destined to endure lifelong punishment, the other for trivial offenders, coincide with the ideas as to future punishment held by some Indian tribes, and especially by the Mandans. Catlin tells us (vol. i. p. 157) that these people believed that their hell, which, like that of the Norsemen, was a cold one, desolate and horrible, covered with eternal ice, was situated far to the north, while the happy hunting-grounds, or their paradise, lay in the south.

We may, perhaps, even dispense with supposing that the oxen seen by Hoei-shin were bison, if we admit that domestic cattle may have existed in America, and been exterminated. Thus, in the " Rélation de Choses de Yucatan de Diégo de Landa," the author tells us that an Indian chief named Cocom showed him one

day an ancient book containing the picture of a common
European cow, and told him it had been prophesied
that when such beasts should come into the country,
the worship of the gods would cease—" Cessario el
culto de los Dioses, y que se avia cumplido, porque los
españoles truxeron vacas grandes." It is true that
this may have been a mere trick of the Indian to flatter
the Spaniard.

D'Eichthal has vindicated Deguignes as regards the
statement that hinds (*biches*) were domesticated in
Fusang, and that cheese was made from their milk, by
citing from the " Popol-Vuh " (Introduction, p. xl.)—
" Milk was known to the Mexicans, who were accustomed
to milk bison-cows and tame hinds, and make cheese."
The statement appears to have been taken from Castañeda.

" The analysis which we have made of the work of
Deguignes," says D'Eichthal, " shows how he availed
himself of the different geographical and historical
documents consulted by him, especially the Chinese
narrative of Fusang. There is, however, in this relation a point which has escaped him; he did not,
and in fact could not, understand who or what those
priests were who, in the 458th year of our era, carried
their doctrines to the country of Fusang; nor did that
other priest, who, forty years later, wrote of that
country." " Formerly," says Deguignes, " these nations
had no knowledge of the religion of Fo. In the year
458 A.C., under the dynasty of *Sum* (Sung), five bonzes

of Samarcand carried their doctrines into this country: then the manners changed" (p. 523).

For Deguignes, as for all men of his time, the religion of Fo was simply one of the national religions of China. Its identity with Buddhism was, I believe, not even suspected. But how could those pretended Chinese bonzes have come from Samarcand? Deguignes, it appears, did not even ask himself this question.

In the time of Klaproth, ideas were more advanced. The identity of the religion of Fo and Buddhism was now acknowledged; and the passage in question is much better translated—" Formerly the religion of Buddha did not exist in those countries. It was in the fourth year, *la-ming*, of the reign of Hiao-wou-te, of Souang (458 A.C.), that five *pi-khieou*, or priests of the country of Ki-pin (the ancient Kophen), went to Fusang, and there spread the law of Buddha. They took with them books, holy images, ritual observances, and established habits of monasticism which altered the manners of the inhabitants."

The land of Ki-pin, the ancient Kophen, is now called Bokhara, the country of Samarcand. Samarcand, indeed, at the time of which we are speaking, was one of the great strongholds of Buddhism. It was in the centre of Asia, one part of it touching Persia, another Turkestan—at the opening of all the roads which led from that central point to the northern frontier of China, and to the north-east of Asia and the shores of the Pacific. If Klaproth had admitted that

Fusang was in America, he would have found in this indication an excellent setting-out-point for studying the institutions and monuments of America, and their relations with Asia. He could the more easily have done so, because at that time the journey of Humboldt to New Spain, and also the "Views of the Cordilleras and Andes," had already appeared, and in those works numerous affinities between the various civilisations of America and Eastern Asia were plainly shown. But by his determination to place Fusang on the South-east Coast of Japan, Klaproth not only lost the benefit of the revelations on the subject of Buddhism furnished by the Chinese document, but also found it a stumbling-block. As we have already remarked, he was led to fix the introduction of Buddhism into a Japanese province in the year 458 of our era, whereas he knew and owned that the establishment of Buddhism in Japan did not take place until the year 582. Besides, we must remember that in Klaproth's time the history of Buddhism, though clear, was still very incomplete. The great works of Hodgson, of Turner, of Burnouf, and those which are derived from them, had not yet appeared. That which Deguignes could not even imagine, that which even Klaproth could have accomplished but imperfectly, is now easy. "By summing up all that we now know of the internal development and the distant propagation of Buddhism, we can well understand what may have been the result of its teaching in America, and can judge, from this point of view, the institutions and monuments of ancient American civilisation."

Such is, in brief, the substance of M. D'Eichthal's vindication of Deguignes against the attack of Klaproth, though it would be but just to say that he has added to it a mass of valuable information which should be read by all who take an interest in the subject. Let me, in conclusion, add a word in sincere praise of the very moderate tone of his defence. Those who have read the bitter accusations which other writers have, in a spirit of honest indignation, hurled against Klaproth, will understand and fully agree with me.

THE

LATEST DISCUSSION OF FUSANG.

T. SIMSON, AND DR E. BRETSCHNEIDER.

CHAPTER XIV.

T. SIMSON AND DR E. BRETSCHNEIDER; OR EUROPEANS RESIDING IN CHINA ON FUSANG.

In the " Notes and Queries on China and Japan,'' published at Hong Kong, there appeared in No. 4, April 1869, this communication:—

" BUDDHIST PRIESTS IN AMERICA.

"I see the following statement in a recent home paper:—

" Professor Carl Neumann, of Munich, a diligent student of Chinese antiquities and bibliography, has discovered from the Chinese Year-Books that a company of Buddhist priests entered this vast continent, *via* Aliaska, a thousand years before Columbus, and explored thoroughly and intelligently the Pacific borders, penetrating into the land of Fusang—for so they called the Aztec territory, after the Chinese name of the Mexican aloe.

" Perhaps some of your numerous contributors may be able to verify the learned sinologue's discovery, and for that purpose I beg to submit it to further inquiry. Y. J. A.

" SHANGHAI, *March* 24, 1869."

In consequence of this request by Y. J. A., there appeared in the next number of the " Notes and Queries for China and Japan " the following letter:—

L

" BUDDHIST PRIESTS IN AMERICA (vol. iii. p. 58).—Under this heading, a querist in the last number of *Notes and Queries* submits to inquiry a statement of Professor Carl Neumann of Munich, respecting the supposed entry of Buddhist priests into the American Continent some thirteen hundred years ago, and their passage into the land of the Aztecs, which they called Fusang, 'after the Chinese name of the American aloe.'

" Now, in the first place, this statement, if true, inferentially proves much more than it asserts ; the Mexican aloe is a native of Mexico only, and it is manifest, therefore, that if these supposed Chinese travellers named the country after the Chinese name of the Mexican aloe, that plant must have been well known to them before the period of their visit to its native country ; hence we are carried further back, to a time when the Mexican aloe must have been known in China, and we must allow a considerable period for it to have become so well known as to suggest to the travellers a name for a newly-discovered—or, as it must needs have been in this view, a rediscovered country. This consideration takes us back into the question of the original peopling of the American Continent, to the age of stone or bronze, perhaps, which is beyond the intended scope of the querist's quotation.

" At the period when ' the land of Fusang is first mentioned by historians,' China, exclusive of the neighbouring 'barbarous tribes,' over whom she held sway, was not so extensive as she is at present, but comprised only what we should now call the Northern and Central Provinces. Does the Mexican aloe grow in that part of the country at all ? I am inclined to think not, though I cannot speak positively upon the point. In Canton it is said by the Chinese to have been introduced from the Philippine Islands, and is called Spanish (or Philippine) hemp, its fibres being sometimes employed in the manufacture of mosquito nets.

" But the Fusang (or, more correctly, the Fusang 扶桑 tree), as described in Chinese botanical works appears to be a malvaceous plant ; at any rate, whatever it may be, it certainly is *not* the Mexican aloe, or anything similar to it.

" The land of Fusang is described by Chinese authors as being in the Eastern Sea, in the place where the sun rises. Considering the geographical limits of China at the time referred to (some 1300 years ago), surely we need not look further than Japan for a very probable identification of the Fusang country according with this description, which indeed appears to be embodied in the more modern name Jih-pên-kwoh, Japan, which is translatable as the ' Country of the Rising Sun.' It is a matter of fact, too, that Buddhism was introduced into that country some 1300 years ago ; and this by no means extraordinary event is a very much more probable version of the incident referred to than the marvellous story given by Professor Neumann.

" Canton.   Theos. Simson."

The note of Y. J. A., of March 24, 1869, refers rather vaguely to a statement in " home papers," by which I infer that American journals are to be understood. In 1850 I published in the New York *Knickerbocker Magazine*, for the first time, my version of Professor Neumann's little work ; and in 1862 republished in the *Continental Magazine* (N.Y.), which I then edited, the greater portion of it, with additions of my own.   It is probable that the paragraph from the " home paper " cited by Y. J. A. originated in an erroneous inference drawn from a hasty perusal of one of these articles. It is therefore needless to comment on Mr Simson's ignorance of the work which he attacked.   His inference that the giving a name to the maguey by the Buddhist monks infers a long previous acquaintance with the plant, indicates a very slight knowledge of the manner in which names are generally given by newcomers to a strange country, as Professor Neumann has indeed intimated. In North America the number of names thus applied, or misapplied, is incredibly large. For an instance nearer home, we may take our own English gipsies, who call a dog a jackal (*juckal*), a swan by the Persian word for a pelican (*sákka* or *sákku*), and small grain by the Hindu word for rice (*shali-giv*, Hindu *shalita*). Hoei-shin did as the Americans and gipsies have done; having no word for a natural product which was new to him, he heedlessly gave to it the name of a familiar plant which he fancied resembled it. The fact that the plant known to Chinese botanists as the Fusang is malvaceous, and unlike the maguey, conflicts in nothing with the probability that Hoei-shin saw the great American aloe. What the fancied point of resemblance may have been, or what kind of a Chinese Fusang-plant he had in his mind, is of comparatively slight importance. The main point, and the one steadily ignored by all who have opposed the views of Deguignes and Neumann, is this: did not Hoei-shin see in the land of Fusang, and afterwards describe—no matter by what name—a remarkable plant, which is to-day the characteristic plant of the region which he is supposed to have visited. The geographical questions raised by Mr Simson, and the possible identity of Japan with Fusang, have been too carefully considered by M. D'Eichthal to render a further discussion of them necessary.

As for the possible antiquity of the name Fusang,

as applied to the maguey, taking us " back into the age of stone or bronze perhaps, which is beyond the intended scope of the querist's quotation," it should be remarked that the ages of both stone and bronze existed contemporaneously for many centuries on the North American Continent until it was settled by Europeans ; and further, that the age of stone continues to exist among a few tribes, as I have acquaintances who not many years ago witnessed the process of making flint arrow-heads among the Indians of Oregon. I can remember having, when a boy, occasionally seen, among sheaves of arrows bought from the Indians of the plains, a few which were flint-tipped, though these were rare, most of them appearing to have heads made from iron hoops. It is therefore evident, that by transferring the period when the name Fusang was given to the " age of stone or bronze " by no means removes the intended scope of the querist's quotation into an era so remote and obscure as to defy research.

The discussion of the question on its native soil, and in its fatherland, China, did not, however, end here. In the fifth number of the *Chinese Recorder and Missionary Journal*, vol. iii., published at Foochow, October 1870, there appeared an article entitled " Fusang ; or, Who Discovered America ? " by " E. Bretschneider, Esq., M.D." It was as follows :—

" In the May number of the *Chinese Recorder* there is an article reproduced from the *Gentleman's Magazine*, in which it is sought to be proved that the Chinese had discovered America as early as 500 A.D. Simultaneous with this there appears in *Notes and Queries* (vol. iv. p. 19) a short notice on the same subject, in which it is desired to collect and publish all notices concerning Fusang, by which name the Chinese of that time are said to have called the newly-discovered America.

" This supposed discovery of America by Buddhist priests has already been the subject of remarks in *Notes and Queries* (vol. iii. pp. 58, 78). Moreover, this is no new view. The first who advanced this hypothesis was the well-known French sinologist Deguignes. (*Vide* his 'Récherches sur les Navigation des Chinois du côté de l'Asie, Mém. de l'Académie des Inscriptions,' &c., vol. xxviii. pp. 505, 526). Klaproth, in his work ' Annales des Empereurs du Japon,' 1834, p. 4, has already pointed out the mistakes into which Deguignes has fallen.

" Mr Taravey published two *brochures* on the same subject. ' L'Amérique sous le nom de Pays de Fusang, a-t-elle été connue en Asie dés le cinquième siécle de notre ére, dans les grandes annales de la Chine.' The other *brochure* is entitled ' L'Amérique sous le nom de Fusang. Nouvelles preuves que le Pays de Fusang est l'Amérique.' I have not read these dissertations. They are quoted by Andrae and Geiger, 1864, in the ' Bibliotheca Sinologica.' I am also equally unacquainted with the article of Mr Neumann." (To this Dr Bretschneider appends as a footnote — " Since writing the above, I have learned with regret of the death of this eminent Oriental scholar.") " I believe, however, that the Chinese notices about Fusang are all derived from one and the same source, and each and all rest upon the statements of a lying Buddhist priest, Hui-shên, who asserts that he was in Fusang. His stories are found in the ' History of the Liang Dynasty ' (502–556 A.D.), chap. liv., and are reproduced by Ma-tuan-lin, and in other historical works.

" The 'History of the Liang Dynasty' refers, in the same chapter in which Fusang is spoken of, to a number of countries, chiefly islands, which must be placed in the same category as Fusang—

that is to say, the intelligence regarding these countries rests
upon rumours and fables. In order to be able properly to
estimate the accounts relating to Fusang, I shall refer shortly
to these countries. The historian of the Liang dynasty speaks
first of the land of the dwarfs (Chu-ju-kuo), lying to the south of
Japan. Here, probably, the islands of Leu-chew are meant, whose
inhabitants are really of little stature. These accounts regarding
the dwarfs are reproduced from the history of the posterior Han.
The Chinese first became acquainted in the year 605 A.D. with the
Leu-chew Islands. The lands of the naked men (Lo-kuo), and the
black-toothed men (Hei-chi), were reached in a year by a sea-
voyage in a south-easterly direction. The latter intelligence is
also reproduced from the history of the Han, and seems to be
an allusion to the nations which chew betel-nut. Ten thousand
li south-west from this is a country of islands inhabited by
black nasty people with white eyes. Their flesh is nevertheless
very well tasted, and those who sail thither shoot them in order
to eat them. Wên-shên, the country in which the people tattoo
themselves, lies 7000 *li* north-east from Japan. The inhabitants
make large lines upon their bodies, and especially upon their
faces. By a stretch of the imagination, we might suppose the
North American Red Indians to be here meant. It is known,
however, that the Japanese have also the custom of tattooing
themselves.

" Lastly, the country *Tahan* is mentioned as 5000 *li* east of
the above. War is here unknown.[1] According to this information, we should look for Tahan somewhere in the Pacific Ocean,
or still further east. The historians of the Tang dynasty, 618–
907, however, assign this land to a place in the middle of
Siberia. The following is found in the 唐 書 chapter 259 b.

" ' The land Tahan is rich in sheep and horses. These, and
likewise the men, are of great stature. Hence the name Tahan.

---

[1] This statement is made from other sources regarding the Esquimaux
by Sir John Lubbock, " Prehist. Civ."

At the lake *Kien-hai* (Baikal, according to Father Hyacinth), the countries of Kie-kia-ssǔ and Kü. The first, according to Klaproth (' Tableaux Historiques de l'Asie ') and others, were the Hakas, the ancestors of the present Kirghises, and dwelt in the present Siberian government of Tomsk and Yenissey. They formed at the time of the Tang dynasty a powerful country. The country of the Kü is described as richly wooded. ' No grass, much moss. There are neither sheep nor horses. On this account stags are used as domestic animals, and harnessed to carts (sledges). They are fed with moss. The people are clothed with stag-skins.' The Chinese historian adds to this, that the people of Tahan had no early intercourse with the Chinese. It was only in the first half of the seventh century that envoys from there came to the Chinese court, and brought sables and horses. According to the above, Tahan must have been a country on the Lena and Yenissey rivers.

"The above - mentioned Buddhist priest, Hui-shên, who arrived in China towards the end of fifth century, relates :—

" ' The kingdom of Fusang lies 20,000 *li* east from Tahan, and directly east from China. The name of the country is derived from the tree of this name (Fusang), which grows there in abundance. Its leaves resembles those of the tree T'ung. The young sprouts are like those of the bamboo, and are eaten. The fruit resembles a pear, and is of a red colour. Cloth is made out of the bark, and paper is also prepared from it. The houses are built of planks. There are no cities. Arms and war are unknown. There are two prisons in the country for light and confirmed criminals. Carts drawn by horses ; oxen or stags are employed. The deer are their domestic animals, like cows in China. A fermented drink is prepared from their milk. Mulberry-trees exist, and red pears, which can be preserved for a whole year. Grapes thrive also. Silver and copper have no value there. There is no iron, but plenty of copper. They possess writings. The inhabitants of Fusang were formerly ignorant of the Buddhist religion. Five priests from Ki-pin

(Cabul) went there in 458 A.D., and carried with them the holy books and the faith.' I pass over the wonderful descriptions which Hui-shên gives of the customs, clothing of the soverèign, punishment, &c., in Fusang, as unessential, for I believe that no conclusions can be drawn therefrom. The translation of these details is found in Klaproth's 'Annales des Empereurs du Japon,' v.

" The above is the Chinese intelligence about Fusang, which sprang out of the fifth century, and, I believe, the only information we possess. In later times, the Chinese poets, who seem to be gifted with a much livelier imagination than some of our *savants*, have further developed and richly embellished those reports with regard to the land of Fusang, and have made out of it a complete land of fables, where mulberry-trees grow to a height of several thousand feet, and where silk-worms are found more than six feet in length. The statements about Fusang given by M. Léon de Rosny in his 'Variétés Orientales,' from a Japanese Encyclopædia, are probably borrowed from the Chinese. I have not, however, read M. Rosny's work. (Cf. *Notes and Queries,* vol. iv. p. 19.) [1]

" In order to place the credibility of the Buddhist priest Hui-shên in the proper light, I will yet mention what he further relates of his journeys. He asserts, namely (*loco citato*), that there is a kingdom 1000 *li* east of Fusang in which are no men, but only women, whose bodies are completely covered with hair. When they wish to become pregnant, they bathe themselves in a certain river. The women have no mammæ, but tufts of hair on the neck, by means of which they suckle their children.

" Upon these vague and incredible traditions of a Buddhist monk, several European *savants* have based the hypothesis that the Chinese had discovered America 1300 years ago. Neverthe-

---

[1] M. de Rosny's extract from the Japanese Cyclopædia is simply an abridgment of the account by Hoei-shin.—C. G. L.

less, it appears to me that these sinologues have not succeeded in robbing Columbus of the honour of having discovered America. They might have spared themselves the writing of such learned treatises on this subject. It appears to me that the verdict passed upon the value of the information of the Buddhist monk Hui-shên by Father Hyacinth is the most correct. This well-known sinologue adds the following words merely after the translation of the article ' Fusang ' out of the ' History of the Southern Dynasties : ' ' Hui-shên appears to have been a consum-mate humbug.' (Cf. 'The People of Central Asia,' by F. Hyacinth.)

"I cannot, indeed, understand what ground we have for be-lieving that Fusang is America. We cannot lay great stress upon the asserted distance, for every one knows how liberal the Chinese are with numbers. By tamed stags we can at all events only understand reindeer. But these are found as frequently in Asia as in America. Mention is also made of horses in Fusang. This does not agree at all with America, for it is well known that horses were first brought to America in the sixteenth century. Neumann appears to base his hypothesis on the assumption that the tree Fusang is synonymous with the Mexican aloe. Mr Sampson has already refuted this error. (*Notes and Queries,* vol. iii. p. 78.)

" According to the description and drawings of the tree Fusang given by the Chinese, there is no doubt that it is a Malvacea. In Peking, the *Hibiscus rosa siniensis* is designated by this name, while *Hibiscus syriacus* is here called Mu-kin. These names seem to hold good for the whole of China. The description which is given in the Pun-tsáo-kang-mu of both plants (xxxvi. p. 64 and 65) admits of no doubt that by the tree Fusang, Chu-kin, Chi-kin, Ji-ki, is to be understood *Hibiscus rosa siniensis.* It is also mentioned that this tree has a likeness to the Mu-kin (*Hibiscus syriacus*). Its leaves resemble the mulberry-tree. Very good drawings of both kinds of *Hibiscus* are found in the Chi-wu-ming-shi-tu-k'ao (xxxv. pp. 58 and 34). The Buddhist priest Hui-shên compares the tree Fusang with the tree T'ung. Under this name the Chinese denote different large-leaved trees. In the Chi-wu-ming-shi-tu-k'ao (xxx. p. 46), the tree T'ung is represented with broadly ovate, cordate, entire great leaves, and with great ovoid, acuminate fruits. Hoffman and Schultes ('Noms indigénes des Plantes du Japon et de la Chine') have set down the tree T'ung as *Paulownia imperialis*. This agrees quite well with the Chinese drawing.

"The tree T'ung must not be confounded with the Yu-t'ung tree (synonyma Ying-tsŭ-t'ung, Jĕn-t'ung), from whose fruit is furnished the well-known and very poisonous oil, Túng-yn, which the Chinese employ in varnish and in painting. It should be the *Dryanda cordata*, according to others *Elaeococca verucosa*. I have not seen the tree, but it is known to occur very abundantly in Central China, and especially on the Yang-tse-kiang. There is a Chinese description in the Pun-tsao (xxxv. p. 26), and a drawing of it in the Chi-wu-ming-shi-tu-k'ao (xxxv. p. 26).

"*Finally*, there is a tree which the Chinese call Wu-t'ung (synonyme Chên). This tree has already been mentioned by Du Halde ('Description de l'Empire Chinois'), as a curiosity, in which the seeds are found on the edges of the leaves. This phenomenon is also described in the drawing of the Chi-wu-ming-shi-tu-k'ao (xxxv. 56). Compare further the description in the Pun-t'sao (xxxv *a*, 25). It is the *Sterculia plantanifolia*, a beautiful tree with large leaves, lobed so as to resemble a hand, which is cultivated in the Buddhist temples near Peking. The Chinese are quite right in what they relate about the seeds. The seed-follicles burst, and acquire the form of coriaceous leaves, bearing the seeds upon their margin.

"The leaves of all the trees just now mentioned allow themselves to be compared, as is done by the Chinese, with those of *Hibiscus*, or other plants of the Malvaceous family, but have not the slightest resemblance with the Mexican aloe or maguey tree (*Agave americana*), which has massive, spiny-toothed, fleshy leaves. Mr Hanlay (*Chinese Recorder*, vol. ii. p. 345), of San

Francisco, cannot, therefore, succeed in proving that the Buddhist priest Hui-shên understood by Fusang the Mexican aloe.

"*Finally*, I have to mention a tree which, as regards its appearance and usefulness, corresponds pretty much with the description given by Hui-shên of the Fusang-tree. I am speaking of the useful tree *Broussonetia papyrifera*, which grows wild *in the temperate parts of Asia*,[1] especially in China, Japan, Corea, Manchuria, &c., and is, besides, found on the islands of the Pacific, while, as far as I know, it does not occur in America. The leaves of this tree are remarkable for their varying very much in shape. The same tree produces at once very large and quite small leaves. They are sometimes entire, sometimes many-lobed. The fruit is round, of a deep scarlet colour, and pulpy. It is a well-known fact that, in the parts where this tree grows, its bark is used for the making of paper and the manufacturing of clothing material. From ancient times it has been known to the Chinese under the name Ch'u (synonyma *Kou*, KOU-SANG, Kou-shu. Cf. Pun-t'sao-kang-mu, xxxvi. 10). An excellent engraving of the tree is found in the Chi-wu-ming-shi-tu-k'ao (xxxiii. 57). *Hui-shên, in his botanical diagnosis, perhaps made a mistake with regard to the Fusang-tree, and confounded Broussonetia with Hibiscus.*

"Just as little as the Mexican aloe does the non-existence of iron in the country Fusang prove that America is to be understood, for there were many countries in ancient times which possessed copper, but where the art of working iron was unknown. The Chinese report also that the natives of the Leu-chew Island did not possess iron, but only copper.

"Mr Hanlay (*l.c.*) appears to have received the discovery of America by the Chinese with the greatest enthusiasm. Perhaps I have furnished him, by means of the above notice about the kingdom of women, *which Hui-shên visited*, a new proof for his

---

[1] Saghalien, where Mr Bretschneider would put Fusang, can hardly be called *temperate*.—C. G. L.

view of the case. Fusang lies, according to Hui-shên, directly east from China more than 20,000 *li*, thus about the situation of San Francisco at the present day. The celebrated women's kingdom lies 1000 *li* still further towards the east, thus about the country of Salt Lake City, where, at the present day, the Mormons are, which, if not a women's country, is nevertheless a country of many women, and where—to the disgrace of the United States—prostitution is carried on under the mask of the Christian religion.

" I do not agree with Mr Sampson (*Notes and Queries*, vol. iii. p. 79) in supposing that Fusang must be identified with Japan, 日本 *Ji-pen*, the land where the sun rises ; *for Japan has been well known to the Chinese since several centuries before our era*, under another name. I avail myself of this opportunity to add a few words about the earliest accounts which the Chinese have of Japan. This country was primitively known to them under the name Wo, which occurs for the first time in the history of the posterior Han, 25–221, chapter 115. I cannot afford to give here a translation of the whole article, and shall, therefore, only touch upon some of the most important points. The kingdom Wo, it is said, is situated on a group of islands in the great sea, south-east of Han (in the south-western part of Corea), and is composed of about a hundred principalities. Since the conquest of Chas-sien (Corea) by the Emperor Wu-ti, 108 B.C., about thirty of these principalities entered into relations with China. The most powerful of the rulers has his capital in Ye-ma-t'ai. It is mentioned that neither tigers and leopards, nor oxen, horses, sheep, and magpies exist. As far as I know, this last remark is not true at present, at least, as far as horses and oxen are concerned ; it is true, however, that sheep cannot thrive in Japan, and the attempts of Europeans to acclimatise them have been, until now, unsuccessful.

" In the reign of Kuang-wu, A.D. 25–58, envoys came from the Wo-nu with presents to the Chinese court. They stated that their country was the southernmost of the kingdom.

" The history of the Sui dynasty, 589–618, chapter 81, gives also the name Wo to Japan, and contains an extensive article on this country. The chief place of the kingdom is called here Ye-mi-sui.

" The name Ji-pên is given to Japan by Chinese historians, for the first time, towards the end of the seventh century. I entertained until now the opinion that the Japanese, who, as everybody knows, use these same signs for the name of their country, but pronounce them *Ni-pon*, had borrowed this name, together with the art of writing, from China. (Chinese writing was introduced into Japan A.D. 280 ; Buddhism, A.D. 552.) (Cf. Klaproth, ' Annales des Empereurs du Japon,' ix. and p. 20.) For Japan could appear only to the Chinese (or any other people on the continent of Asia) as the country where the sun rises. This, however, does not seem to be the case, according to information derived from Chinese sources.   In the history of the T'ang dynasty, 618–907, chapter 259 *a*, Japan is at first described under the ancient name Wo.   Then follows the description of the kingdom Ji-pên, of which the following is said :—' Ji-pên is of the same origin as Wo.   It lies on the boundaries of the sun, therefore the name.'   It is also related that the name Wo was changed by the Japanese, for the reason that they found it inharmonious ; others say that Ji-pên was formerly a small state, and that Wo, in later times, was incorporated in Ji-pên.   The people who came from Ji-pên to the court boasted of the power of their country, but the Chinese did not put faith in their words.   They told that this kingdom extended 1000 *li* in all directions, and that it was bordered on the west and south by the great sea, and on the north and east by high mountains. Beyond the mountains live the Mas-jen, the hairy men.   This, beyond doubt, refers to the Ainos, well known for being hairy in appearance.

" The above information removes all doubts as to the Japanese origin of the name Ji-pên, and the use of it at first for the designation of the largest of the islands, and afterwards as the name of the whole empire. Ye-ma-t'ai, as the Chinese called the chief town of Japan, seems to designate the province Yamato, in which the emperors had their residence in ancient times. It is difficult to say anything of the origin of the name Wo. It is probable that the Chinese invented it, and that the Japanese afterwards adopted it. I find in a Japanese historical map of Japan the characters 大倭 as designating the province Yamato. This province is designated by these characters on all the historical maps up to the beginning of the eighth century, whereas on the modern maps that province is called 大和 Taho.

" Allow me to observe also, in relation to the above-mentioned history of the posterior Han, a Nü-wang-kuo, a country of women, is spoken of in the southern part of Japan. This statement is confirmed by the Japanese annals. (Cf. Klaproth, 'Annales des Empereurs du Japon,' p. 13.) The Japanese call this country Atsowma.

" The land Tahan, according to the foregoing observations, must have been a province in Siberia. Fusang is said to lie to the east of Tahan. Supposing, then, that a country, Fusang, really existed, and was not an invention of a Buddhist monk, it does not necessarily follow that it is to be sought on the other side of the ocean. Let me here observe, that this monk mentions in no place in his account having passed over a great sea. Klaproth, in assuming that Fusang is meant for the island of Saghalien, is, I believe, more near to the truth than the other sinologues.

" In *Notes and Queries* (vol. iv. p. 19) there is a passage cited out of the Liang-ssŭ-kung-ki, that the kingdom of Fusang had sent envoys to China. That would, of course, prove that the so-called country of Fusang had political intercourse with China, but it makes it more unlikely that America was here meant. We will, *therefore,* in the meantime, still consider Fusang as a *terra incognita nec non dubia,* and bestow upon Mr Burlinghame the double honour of having been the first American Ambassador at the Chinese court, and first Chinese Ambassador in America.

" The contradictory fancies about China that originate in the brains of European literati are truly astonishing. Some maintain that the Chinese discovered America 1300 years ago, while a well-known learned Frenchman, Count Gobineau, has some years ago asserted that the Chinese have immigrated from America. In his 'Essai sur l'Inégalité des Races Humaines,' vol. ii. p. 242, Count Gobineau says :—'D'où venaient ces peuples jaunes ? Du grand continent d'Amérique. C'est la réponse de la physiologie comme de la linguistique.'

" All these unfounded hypotheses have much the same value as the supposed discovery of America by the Chinese.

"Pekin, 13*th June* 1870."

As a Chinese scholar, familiar with the histories of the country, and as a resident in Pekin at the time of writing the foregoing letter, Dr. Bretschneider is entitled to an examination in detail. Beyond all doubt, no writer whatever on the subject of Fusang, whether Deguignes, Neumann, or D'Eichthal, has expressed himself so positively on the question. A true disciple of the learned Klaproth, he with great ingenuity directs his chief energies less to the subject of dispute than to impugning the honesty or sense of his opponents.

In the beginning, Dr Bretschneider disposes of all that Deguignes alleges, by declaring that " Klaproth has already pointed out the mistakes into which the latter has fallen." By this effective summary, those who have not read Deguignes and Klaproth are fully informed in a few words of the greater part of the argument—as it appeared to Dr Bretschneider ; and as he had not read Professor Neumann's or other works on the subject, he is, of course, relieved from the awkward responsibility of answering many statements which would perhaps have interfered with his own theories. As he makes no mention, indeed, of M. Gustave d'Eichthal, we must conclude that he either had never heard of the articles which had appeared several years before in the *Révue Archæologique*, or passed them by as trifles unworthy his attention.

" The Chinese notices of Fusang," says Dr Bretschneider, " are all derived from the same source, and each and all rest upon the statements of a lying Buddhist priest." He does not deny, or he rather admits plainly, that the steps towards Fusang are laid down faithfully enough until we reach Tahan. No one, indeed, can well deny this who has read Deguignes with any care. But the credibility of Hoei-shin is utterly destroyed, according to Dr Bretschneider, firstly, by the stories embroidered by Chinese poets on his narrative hundreds of years after the monk was in his grave, and, secondly, by the story of the Kingdom of Women.

I have already observed that Hoei-shin says nothing of having visited this Kingdom of Women, but speaks of it as being a thousand *li* east of Fusang. In our day, it is no longer the fashion to utterly discredit the older travellers because they gilded and illuminated their texts with arabesque marvels, especially when they only told the tales as they were told to them. Judged by such a standard, all the travels of Buddhist

M

monks to the West must be entirely thrown out of
history, Herodotus set down as the father of lies, and
every one of the Old World pilgrims discredited with
him.   In fact, the *falsus in uno falsus in omnibus*
ground no longer obtains in criticism, and allowance is now made for the simple credulity of twilight
times.   Scholars do not usually announce their personal opinions as overwhelming arguments, or call
names, and it is to be regretted that a man of Dr
Bretschneider's erudition should have informed the
sinologues who differ with him that "they might have
spared themselves the trouble of writing such learned
treatises on this subject."   That he likes this method
of argument by inspiration spiced with personality
appears from his evident admiration of Father Hyacinth, who, as he tells us, *merely* added to the article
" Fusang " the following words—" Hui-shên appears to
have been a consummate humbug."

Dr Bretschneider adduces the story of the Kingdom
of Women as a reason for discrediting Hoei-shin.   Yet,
when it strengthens his own position, he informs us that
a country of women was believed to exist in Southern
Japan.

"Neumann," says Dr Bretschneider, "appears to
base his hypothesis on the assumption that the tree
Fusang is synonymous with the American aloe."   As
he confessedly had not read Professor Neumann's work,
it was hardly fair to judge by hearsay, or to inform
his public (even under the shield of an " appears ")

what Neumann's "hypothesis" was. The reader of
these pages is aware that Professor Neumann by no
means based his belief in Hoei-shin's narrative simply
on the maguey plant. "Mr Sampson," says Dr Bretschneider, "has already refuted this error." Mr Simson had, it is true, fully proved that Hoei-shin gave to
the maguey a name not now applicable to the Chinese
plants which bear it. But neither Mr Simson nor
Dr Bretschneider disproves the *main* fact—that Hoei-
shin described a very singular Mexican plant not
known in Asia. The pictures which have been made
by Chinese botanists since the fifth century are very
little to the purpose. It seems to have escaped the notice
of all writers that Hoei-shin, while he calls the tree a
Fusang, says it resembles the T'ung,[1] a very different
plant, the leaves of which, though in other respects unlike those of the maguey, are large. This indicates that
by the word Fusang we are to understand some American term, which to the Chinese sounded like one already
familiar to them. And it is remarkable that one point
—and that, indeed, the principal one in the Fusang con-
troversy—has been overlooked by every writer on the
subject, from Deguignes to Bretschneider, which is, that
Hoei-shin, while he calls the tree a Fusang, states that its

---

[1] A cactus in ancient Mexican was called *tuna*, and the *Cactæ globosæ*
bears the name of *visnago* (*vide* Berthold Seeman's "Die Volksnamen der
Amerikanischen Pflanzen," or "Popular Names of the Plants of America");
but I have not been able to learn that there is any old Mexican name for
the maguey in the least resembling Fusang. Inquiry might be made
among the Pueblos.

leaves resemble those of another plant, and its sprouts
those of yet another. It is not remarkable that, with these
qualifications left out of sight, neither Mr Simson nor
Dr Bretschneider could find the mysterious plant among
the Fusang-trees of China. Nothing can be more plain
than that, while giving to the American plant a name like
that of one in China, the monk by no means meant the
latter. "The sprouts," he says, "*on the contrary*,
resemble those of the bamboo-tree." Yet in the face
of this statement, Mr Simson and Dr Bretschneider
assert, as if it were an argument, that the maguey plant
is *not* the Fusang—when the monk had taken pains to
say the same thing, and even to emphasise his denial.
But, as a concluding paragraph on this subject, Dr
Bretschneider informs us that there is a Chinese tree—
not the Fusang but Kousang—which strikingly resembles it, and then naively remarks that this was perhaps the one seen by Hoei-shin. The correction will
be cheerfully admitted by all who believe it possible
that the Buddhist monk was in America; and I avail
myself of the opportunity to declare that Dr Bretschneider, whatever his peculiarities of criticism may
be, is undoubtedly a good sinologist, and deeply learned
in Chinese botany, and that his learning has, in this
respect, done much for the cause of Hoei-shin, while his
arguments *pro contra* have not injured it in the least.
Hoei-shin in all likelihood did make a mistake in con-
founding *Broussonetia* with *Hibiscus*; but so that there
is in China a Kousang, very much resembling what the

monk chose to call Fusang, we can ask no more. Dr Bretschneider honestly admits that Hoei-shin saw in Mexico a plant to which he gave a wrong name, and corrects this error. To an unprejudiced critic these botanical blunders of the old monk, obscured in all probability by provincial terms and errors of copyists, so far from invalidating the main facts, actually confirm them; and in this instance, where Dr Bretschneider is inspired by positive science, he makes an admission favourable to the credibility of Hoei-shin.

It is, however, strange that so learned a man should assert that because there were in ancient times many other countries where iron was unknown, therefore Hoei-shin's observation that it was not used in Fusang must go for nothing. Iron was known to all the civilised countries with which Hoei-shin was acquainted—what his ideas of Lew-chew were we cannot ascertain—and when he found in Fusang an apparently civilised race without iron, *and not using gold or copper for money*, he naturally recorded these peculiarities. It is remarkable that this was the case in Mexico. Four statements are here made—one relative to a plant, and three to metals —all of them true as regards America, and not one of them confirmed as regards China or India in the fifth century. According to Dr Bretschneider's argument, the most accurate account of the inhabitants of America, and their customs, must be set down as proving nothing, whenever anything similar can be proved of other coun- tries in ancient times.

Dr Bretschneider states that Hoei-shin declares he visited the Kingdom of Women; but, as I have already shown, the monk uses the term "it is said" with reference to the great marvel of this country—the extraordinary manner of suckling the children—which he would not have done had he witnessed it. And here we are again indebted to Dr Bretschneider for another inadvertent, yet most important, admission. For, as he declares, Fusang lies—according to Hoei-shin—more than 20,000 *li* directly east from China, about the situation of San Francisco; and that the Women's Kingdom, if it existed, must have been where the Mormons now dwell. Now the question on which the whole turns is really this, and nothing more:—Did Hoei-shin mean that there was a country on the spot where, as is now known, land exists? The monk had a perfect right to state his distances, and here Dr Bretschneider clearly admits that the distance was accurately estimated. It may be remarked, by the way, that prostitution has literally no existence in Utah, being vigorously repressed by the Mormons, and that our author has evidently been strangely misinformed as to the country. It is carried on, he says, under the mask of the Christian religion, an assertion which would be perfectly true if applied to Berlin or Paris, or in fact to any German or French city where it is legalised by the Government, but which cannot be said of the United States of America, and least of all of Utah, where the people are not Christians at all. It would be insulting to a scholar like Dr Bretschneider to insinuate that he does not know the difference between prostitution and polygamy. I prefer to believe that he wrote under a misapprehension of Mormon institutions. If, however, we are to understand from Dr Bretschneider's text that he alludes to the American Government as wearing a mask of the Christian religion, I would say, as an American, firstly, that the expression is needlessly offensive; and secondly, that as there is no connection whatever in the United States between Church and State, it is devoid of truth.

"Klaproth," says Dr Bretschneider, "in assuming that Fusang is meant for the Island of Saghalien, is, I believe, more near to the truth than the other sinologues." What then becomes of the perplexing Country of Women—but just now in Utah, and at another time in Japan? If anybody's statements and measurements are to be accepted, they are certainly those of Hoei-shin himself, and they are plain enough—"Twenty thousand *li* east of Tahan"—Tahan being plainly Siberia, as Dr Bretschneider admits, when he finds it convenient to do so, for the sake of a bitter word against America.

A passage cited from an old Chinese chronicle asserts that envoys once went from Fusang to China. This, Dr Bretschneider allows, would prove that Fusang had intercourse with the Celestial Kingdom, "but," as he declares, "makes it still more unlikely that America was here meant." In explanation, I will

cite the passage as given in the " Notes and Queries for
China and Japan."

" The ' Liang-sze-kung-ki' says that envoys from Fusang brought as tribute ' gems for observing the sun,'
like square and circular mirrors, more than a foot in
circumference, and transparent like glass.   Looking at
the reflection of the sun in them, one could see very
distinctly and brightly the palace in the sun." [1]

This refers distinctly enough to something very like
those curious metallic mirrors made in China, and
common even in London, by means of which characters
or pictures on the back are seen by reflecting the sun's
rays on the wall.   But in any case, if such mirrors
were ever brought to China, they were much more likely
to have come from sun-worshipping Mexico, where
metal and other work was made with great ingenuity,
than from Siberia, or even from Japan itself at that
time.   But it is still utterly incomprehensible why
the proving that Fusang sent ambassadors to China

[1] The ancient Peruvians are said by Prescott to have relighted their
sacred fire when it was extinguished by means of a concave *mirror* of
polished metal.   This connection between mirrors and the sun, whether
Chinese or Peruvian, is at least curious.   Not only Peruvians, but many
of the North American nations, preserved a sacred fire—in fact, the Pueblos of New Mexico still keep one burning, and it is not many years since
the Chippeways extinguished theirs.   I have in my possession a common
burning-glass, which I once dug out of an old Chippeway grave ; and it is
to be observed that burning-glasses, which were in great demand from the
traders by the Chippeways while they worshipped the sacred fire, are
now no longer called for.   This is not owing to the introduction of
matches, for (as is proved by the contents of several tobacco-bags in my
possession) the Chippeways generally use flint and steel to obtain a light.
—C. G. L.

should " *make it still more unlikely* that America is here meant." There is no reason to arbitrarily assume that ambassadors could not come from America. But Dr Bretschneider treats this as his most conclusive argument ; indeed, as the only conclusive one, since he immediately declares, " We will *therefore* still consider Fusang as a *terra incognita nec non dubia."*

In brief, Dr Bretschneider asserts that there was no Fusang, it being all the invention of a lying priest —but that it was in Siberia. There was never any such place, but still Mr Simson is wrong in placing it in Japan, and Klaproth is right in declaring it was at Saghalien. There was no Fusang-tree either, but the monk who saw it meant the *Kou*-sang, describing more accurately, however, a Mexican plant. Klaproth refuted Deguignes and exposed his errors by proving that Fusang was also in Japan ; only in Dr Bretschneider's opinion it was elsewhere. And it is certainly curious that the writers who utterly discredit the very existence of Fusang, and all that is said of it, have each a theory as to where it really was.

To verify history is the chief object of scholarship, just as to investigate Nature is the aim of science. Every year sees the former more guided by the latter, and it is well that it should be so, even as it is well that parents who, as they grow old, look more and more into the past, should be tenderly guarded by their vigorous children. To prove who first from the Old World explored the New is no trifling problem in history, and

I am well assured that the investigation of the record of Hoei-shin will by no means rest where it is. What we want is not to establish a favourite fancy, but to ascertain the truth. It does not appear to many people, whose opinions are entitled to respect, that the story of Hoei-shin is settled. Liars—above all, lying travellers— are never brief, and had Hoei-shin been " a consummate humbug," he would have hardly left such a concise narrative as is given in the Annals. Time will proba- bly show whether these Buddhist monks ever existed, and whether they ever were in America—

> " The truth, which long in darkness lay,
> Will come with clearness to the day."

And if their story be proved a misrepresentation, or a myth founded on some old fable, we may at least get from the inquiry set afoot a clue to its source, and hints, or perhaps solid information, as to the great mystery of the early settlement of America. We are still groping in darkness as regards the past: the wonderful discoveries of the last fifty years may well teach us this.

It is the impulsive—it may be the credulous—spirit, loving marvels and novelty, which awakes these re- searches, and the negative, doubting, and incredulous inquiry which tests them. I trust that in this book both the believers and disbelievers in Hoei-shin's nar- rative have been honestly represented. If I have inadvertently spoken harshly of Klaproth and his dis- ciple Bretschneider, I can only say that my severest words are like flattery itself compared to what others have said in print of both these scholars. As it is, I cannot resist the honest conviction that both have, by their opposition, kept the question from subsiding into oblivion, and unwittingly brought forth, if not positive proofs, at least a mass of probabilities in favour of Hoei-shin before which their opposition was trifling.

The truth is, that the vindication of Hoei-shin is of little importance in itself compared to what lies behind it and what it may lead to. I refer to those early ages peopled by strange and cloudy forms—ages not without gleams of barbaric splendour—hinted at in the account of the embassies bearing mirrors in which could be seen " the palace of the sun "—perhaps that very Palace of the Sun itself known so well to the Mexicans. Should the investigation lead to anything positive relative to the early settlement of America, and to the action or reaction of the Old World and the New, the little journal of the humble priest, who did not even claim to be the first from beyond sea whose footsteps had fallen in the Golden Land of Fusang, may well be allowed to pass into oblivion, if nothing more occurs to confirm its authenticity.

APPENDIX.

———◇———

In the text of Professor Neumann's work, there is an extract from the *Nipponski*, or Japanese Annals (from 661 until 696), relative to the Ainos, or inhabitants of Jeso. As anything concerning these inter-continental races is of interest in connection with the subject of this work, especially when it refers to any possible affinity between America and Asia, I append the following from the London *Times* (Nov. 1874) :—

The Ainos of Japan.—Mr De Long, lately United States Minister in Japan, made the following statement in his lecture at Sacramento : — " The Japanese estimate their population at about 40,000,000. This I think an over-estimate by from 10,000,000 to 15,000,000, although their reckoning is supported by their census returns. There is found inhabiting the island of Jeso and the Kurile Islands a race of men called by the Japanese ' Ainos,' or ' hairy men.' This appellation they well sustain, as they have full, flowing, black beards, reaching, in many cases, below the middle of the breast. We are told that they are the aborigines of Japan, originally occupying all of the islands embraced in that group ; and Japanese history records the fact that Jimoo Tenno, the first Japanese emperor, with some followers, came from heaven in a boat, landed at or near Nagasaki, on the Island of Sikoke, from whom sprang the present Japanese nation ; that gradually they beat back and destroyed the Aino race, as we have done the Indian, until the nation attained its present greatness, and the aborigines sank to their present weak condition. This is all the Japanese know of their origin and their race. Nothing interests their leading men more than a study of their probable origin, as they treat with levity the legend recorded in their country. The embassy which accompanied me to Washington brought with them a large collection of stone beads, arrow-heads, and other evidences of the stone age. These they brought for the purpose of comparing them with similar relics found in our own and other countries. The embassy studied with great regard such Indians as we met, and such relics as could be found at Salt Lake City and other places. Iwakura assured me that the appearance of our Indians, their dress, costume, and weapons, were identical with such ornamentation as their geologists had discovered upon rude images marking the stone age in Japan ; and he further remarked to me that he would be almost prepared to believe they were akin, but for the circumstance that our Indians could not be civilised. The Ainos form, in my mind, a curious subject of reflection. They seem to bear no relation in customs, language, or appearance to either the Japanese, Chinese, Manchoos, or other Oriental nations. They are extremely kind, mild-mannered, skilful as hunters and fishermen, intelligent, and brave. Crime is almost unknown among them, yet they are so completely savage or barbarous that they have no idea of their origin, no mode of reckoning time, no knowledge of the value of money, nor even proper names. They call their children ' One,' ' Two,' ' Three,' &c. Their mode of saluting a superior is to sit down upon the earth cross-legged, bow the head, and, placing their hands together with the palms upward, raise them three times toward their faces, as if in the act of casting dust or water upon themselves, after which they complacently stroke their long black beards with both hands three times. This mode of salutation, I believe, is analogous to that of the ancient Hebrews, while the beard and physiognomy of the people, in my mind, strongly resemble that nation. Ancient mining works of a very extensive character are found upon the island of Jeso, where these people live, and are mentioned by Professor Pompelly, who resided there for a period, while in the service of the Japanese, in his work entitled ' A Tour Around the World.' "

This interest of the Japanese in early America, and their belief that their ancestors had something in common with it, is possibly more deeply seated than Europeans are aware of. In his " New Japan," Mr Samuel Mossman, author of " China and its History," &c., writes as follows on this subject :—

" There is evidence to show that some of the early Japanese navigators, driven by the terrible typhoons that sweep over their waters, had entered the great North Pacific drift current flowing to the east—as observed by Krusenstern and Kotzebue—and reached the coasts of California and Mexico. They could not return again to their native land against the current, so those involuntary explorers were in all probability the founders of the Mexican dynasties, of which the famous Montezuma was among the last monarchs. When Cortes arrived in Mexico, he was received by the king and his sages as one whom they expected from the land of their ancestors in the *far distant west.* Hence it may be said that the Japanese were the first discoverers and founders of America. Even at this day, the remnants of the aboriginal races of California and Mexico have been recognised by intelligent natives from Japan as descendants of their ancestors, whose boats had been carried by currents or driven by tempests from their native shores."

This is an interesting subject, and I regret that more conclusive proofs than those hinted at by Mr Mossman cannot be given. As the Japanese are, however, intelligent scholars, it is to be hoped that among their traditions or literature something may be found confirming the belief that their ancestors carried civilisation to America.

It has been recently discovered that the Indians of Aliaska, until within a century, made mummies of their dead, and deposited them with arms and carved work in caves which were carefully closed. Should it ever be found that this custom prevails, or ever did prevail, among the Ainos, it would be another presumptive link not without value towards establishing the chain of evidence referring to the ancient union of the Old World with the New.

Since these chapters went to press, I have conversed with a gentleman holding the rank of General in the United States regular army, who has not only passed many years in active intercourse with a great variety of Indian tribes, but has had many opportunities of studying Mongolian types. Among his observations were the following :—Having asked him if he had ever observed a resemblance between Red Indians and Tartars, he replied that he had, but that it was more marked in some tribes than in others. On inquiring in which tribe it was most apparent, he promptly replied the Sioux. Another gentleman who was present confirmed the resemblance, and commented on the former great extent of the Dakotahs. On asking General —— how he accounted for this likeness being stronger in the Indians of the Plains than in the Chippeways, he replied with substantially the same suggestion as that which I have given at the end of Chapter IX. of this work—that all Red Indians, and many Eastern Asiatics, had a common Mongol origin, which in the nomadic and equestrian life of the Plains, had redeveloped itself into a type somewhat resembling that existing in the steppes of Tartary. He also declared that, in all Red Indian tribes, there is a really extraordinary resemblance of squaws to Chinese women. This is recognised by both Indians and Chinese when they meet—as they now very frequently do—in California and Oregon. My informant had been interested and amused at seeing the prompt intimacy which often ensued on such rencontres. Chinese and Red Indian women have in common a very peculiar custom, not found among Aryan races. Many of my American readers will understand to what I allude. I am inclined to believe that Nature manifests herself in these affinities. Once, at an English boat-race on the Thames, I saw a group of gipsies eyeing with intense interest a very dark and very well-dressed gentleman. As I approached, one of them muttered to me in his language, " *Rya ma pensa tu te adovo rye se Romanis ?* " ("Master, don't you think that gentleman is gipsy?") I was under the impression that it was a wealthy Jew from India, who lived in the neighbourhood, and told the Petulengo there was no gipsy blood there. But I found afterwards that the dark gentleman was really Hindoo. An old gipsy woman, when she saw the Shah, declared positively there was something Rommany in him; "she knew it well enough." And as she herself used half-a-dozen Persian words in saying so, I thought her partly right. Gipsies fraternise very readily with natives of India, but not with Jews; nor have I ever heard of Chinese or Red Indians regarding mulattoes as of their blood—with the exception, perhaps, of "Jim Beckworth," whose assertion must, however, be taken with allowance. General —— recognised the custom of love-making described by Hoei-shin in Fusang as common to several Red Indian tribes, though it does not—at present, at least—last so long among the latter as it did in the days of the monk. A month is generally sufficient, in these degenerate days, for the suitor to reside near his love; but the higher the pretensions of the girl, the longer must he continue his residence.

My informant had lived among the Pueblos. He was positive that there were among them *virgins* appointed to keep the sacred fire burning, but added, that there were male priests also charged with the same duty. He had remarked that the Indians of the North-west Coast frequently repeat in their well-known black-stone carvings the dragon, the lotus-flower, and the alligator, specimens of which he had recently given to a well-known professor at Oxford.

It is difficult to touch on the resemblance of North American Indians to inhabitants of Asia, without becoming involved in the differences of opinion between what Daniel Wilson calls the American school of ethnologists, and others in Europe. According to the former, to use the words of Wilson, the American aborigines are affirmed "to constitute one nearly homogeneous race, varying within very narrow limits from the prevailing type, and agreeing in so many essentially distinctive features as to prove them a well-defined, distinct species of the genus *Homo.* Lawrence, Wiseman, Agassiz, Squier, Gliddon, Nott, and Meigs, might each be quoted in confirmation of this opinion, and especially of the prevailing uniformity of certain strongly-marked

N

cranial characteristics ; but the source of all such opinions is the justly-distinguished author of the 'Crania Americana,' Dr Morton of Philadelphia." Mr Wilson holds that this idea of a nearly absolute homogeneity pervading the tribes and nations of the Western Hemisphere, through every variety of climate and country, is so entirely opposed to the ethnic phenomena witnessed in other quarters of the globe, that it is deserving of the minutest investigation.   The marked differences which have been found to exist among the men, as among the fauna peculiar to the Western Hemisphere, are explained by Agassiz as "an indefinite limitation between species," or " a tendency to split into minor groups running really into one another, notwithstanding some few marked differences " ("Indigenous Races of the Earth," p. 14).   Mr Wilson holds that recent researches indicate radical differences among the aborigines of America ; and that, for instance, tried by Dr Morton's own definitions and illustrations, the famous Scioto Valley skull essentially differs from the American typical cranium in some of its most characteristic features. And Mr Wilson further claims that, of a great number of ancient American skulls examined by him, very many exhibited an unmistakable difference from the so-called typical skull of Morton, while a general uniformity is traceable in a considerable number of Mexican crania, " but not without such notable exceptions as to admit of their division also into distinct dolichocephalic and brachycephalic groups."   When it is recognised, as both Morton and Agassiz have done, that there are marked differences between American aboriginal skulls—differences as great as are allowed for different races in Europe—it does not establish their identity to declare they all "run into each other," and are all variations from the Scioto Mound skull.   This, which is characterised by Morton as the perfect type of Indian conformation, to which the skulls of all the tribes, from Cape Horn to Canada, more or less approximate, presents two-thirds of its cerebral mass in front of the *meatus auditorius externus ;* whereas, in the elongated Peruvian skull, unaltered by artificial means, this is almost exactly reversed, showing, by the proportions of the cerebral cavity, that fully two-thirds of the brain lay behind the *meatus auditorius.* The reader who is interested in this subject may consult Mr Wilson's "Prehistoric Man" (London, Macmillan & Co., 1862), for the arguments on either side. *Non nobis tanta componere lites.* But neither view affects the probability of Hoei-shin's having visited America, nor the fact that there are at present regular links of likeness between the American Indians of the North-west Coast through the Aleutian Islands to Asia. That Dr Morton himself had no prejudices on this subject is evident, since he, with the late Albert Gallatin, having read in the MS. my translation of Professor Neumann's work, expressed a great interest in it, and manifested no opposition to the opinions advanced, excepting, indeed, that Dr Morton said to me, in conversation on the subject, that such authority as that of Chinese annals seemed obscure and doubtful. Professor Neumann, as may be seen on referring to his text, fully accepted Dr Morton's views of an entire unity between all the American Indian tribes, but apparently held the opinion that, at some very early age, they had a common origin with certain Asiatic races. At present only one thing is certain, that our knowledge is far from being sufficiently advanced to enable us to decide a question which, when carried out, may involve that of the origin of man.

INDEX.

———◇———

ACOSTA, 136

Affinities of American and Asiatic languages, 99

Agattou and Semitchi Islands, 69

Agave americana, 37, 162, 171

Age of stone or bronze, 162, 165

Ainos or Jebis, extent of the race, 11 ; called Crab Barbarians, *ib.* ; when first described, 12 ; called Hairy People, *ib.* ; embassy to Japan, *ib.*; wars against Japan, 14 ; images of, 22 ; paint themselves, 140 ; same as Mao-jen, 174. *Vide* Appendix.

Akkad, 100

Albert Gallatin on American languages, 156

Alceste Island, 66

Aleutian or Fox Islands, 11, 22, 70

Aliaska on the early maps, 148

Aloe, Mexican, known in China, 162

Amakirima, 67

Amazonia, 29

Ambassadors from Fusang, 184 ; Ambassade des Hollandais, 129 ; first Japanese to China, 173

America, how first populated, 8 ; formation of American races, *ib.*; their unity, *ib.*

American coast, castaways on, 43, 76

Amur or Amoor River, 132 ; Tartars on the, 145

Anahuac, 35

Ancient races of North American Indians, 100 *et seq.*

Ancient records of Mexico, 86

Ancient vessels of North-eastern Asia, 64

Andræ and Geiger, 166

Antecedent probability that Orientals went to America, 59
Aztec god of war, 36 ; computation of time, 39
Aztecs declare they came from the north, 136 ; later accounts of, 33
" Archiv für die wissenschaftliche Kunde von Russland," 149
Arrow-heads made of flint, 165
Atsowma, 175
Attou Island, 68
Avatcha, 146 ; Bay of, 68
Aymara, Peruvian, 100

BAY of St Lawrence, Siberia, 75
Baikal, Lake, 144
Bartlett, John Russell, 151
Beans, Mexican (*frijoles*), 135
Behring's Straits or Anadir, 9
" Bibliotheca Sinologica," 166
Bigandet, Father R. R., 93
Bison and oxen, 153
Black Dragon River, 15
" Book of Mountains and Seas," 12
Brasseur de Bourbourg, L'Abbé, 151
Bretschneider, Dr, his opinion of Hoei-shin, 165 ; his discussion of Fusang,
    ib. ; his opinion of all who believe in Fusang, 169 ; he approves
    of Father Hyacinth's expression, 170 ; Reply to Dr Bretschneider,
    176 ; summary of his argument, 185
Broussonetia papyrifera, 172, 180
Buache, Philip, his map, 126, 147
Buddha, images of, 119 ; attitude of, 120
Buddhism, 4 ; its influence in partly breaking Chinese exclusiveness, 5 ;
    in Fusang, 28 ; its extension, 31 ; introduced into Fusang, 143 ; its
    progress, 113 ; not understood by Deguignes, 155 ; introduced into
    Japan, 156, 163
Buddhist priests in America, discussed by Simson, 162 ; monks, 5 ;
    Trinity, *ib.* ; writings an important part of Chinese literature and
    history, 65 ; travels of, 87
Burlinghame, 175
Burnouf, works of, 156

CACTUS, in ancient Mexican, *tuna,* 119

California, coast of, 147 ; Chinese merchants there in early times, 150

Cape San Lucas, 71

Carpin, Jean du Plan de, 33

Catacualcans, 136

Catlin, 152

Chan-hai-king on Fusang, 143

Chamo, great desert of, 130

Charlevoix, " Histoire de la Nouvelle France," 137

Che-goi tribes, sable hunters, 132 *et seq.*

Chicago, ancient skulls from, 111

Children, change in appearance of, in new climates, 78

Chinese precepts relative to the outer world, 3 ; early embassies, 4 ; reception of envoys, *ib.* ; knowledge of foreign countries, 6 ; pride and vanity, *ib.* ; acquire knowledge of North-eastern Asia, 9 ; Chinese and Japanese in Kamtschatka and the Hawaiian group, 43 *et seq.* ; *Recorder and Missionary Journal,* 165 ; Chinese poets, 169

Chippeway perpetual fire, 184

Chi-tao-an, 89

Chi-wu-ming-shi-tu-k'ao, drawing of *Hibiscus* in the, 170

Chu-kon, Kon-sang, Kon-shu, 172

Chu-kin, Chi-kin, Jiki, synonyms for *Hibiscus rosa siniensis,* 170

Chy-wei Youtché or Youtchy, 144

Cibola, 152

Clavigero, Storia Antica del Messico, 35

Clarke Hyde, Mr, 99

Cocom, Indian chief, shows picture of a cow ; ancient prophecy told by him, 154

Cochran, Lieutenant, 130

Colours applied to cycles of time, 40

Columbus, 75 ; his vessels, 76

Continental Magazine (N.Y.) for 1862 contained a portion of the present work, 163

Cooper, Fenimore, name of vessel, 68, 76

Copper in Fusang, 28, 38

Criminals in Fusang, 46, 47

Currents, the Japanese, 74 ; the Peruvian or Humboldt Current, *ib.*

D'Acosta, 150

Dakota or Sioux language, 101 ; affinity with Ural-Altaic languages, 102 ; resemblance of Dakotas to Tartars, 192

Dead placed in trees by the Tunguse, 10

Deer, 10

Deguignes, Klaproth, and D'Eichthal, 125 ; Deguignes determined that Wenshin was Jeso, 129 ; old writers cited by, *ib.* ; his account of the different people on the route more detailed than Neumann's, 131 ; determined that Fusang was New Mexico, 133 ; remarks on Kingdom of Women, 134 ; his argument, 138 ; wrote according to his title, 139 ; on the second itinerary, 143 *et seq.* ; traces the route, 148 *et seq.* ; cited by Bretschneider, 166

D'Eichthal, his memoir, 125, 127 *et seq.* ; his defence of Deguignes, 125 *et seq.* ; observations on Aleutian Islands, 132 ; on distance from Tahan, 140

De Laët, 127 ; describes Pueblo Indians, 136

De Landa, Diego de, on Yucatan, 153

De Long, Mr, on the Ainos and Japanese, 188

Delaware Indians called women, 134

De l'Isle, M. Guillaume, 147

"Description of Western Countries," a Chinese work destroyed in Pekin, 89

Distance between Corea and middle of Niphon, 140 ; from China to Fusang, as claimed by the believers in Hoei-shin, fully admitted by Dr Bretschneider, 182

Djourdje, ancestors of the present Mongols, 144

Dogs, swine, devils, and savages, Chinese names for races of the north, south, east, and west, 6 ; dogs in Kamtschatka, 20 ; dog smelling land, 73

Domestic animals in Fusang, 40

Dryanda cordata, 171

Eastern and Central Asiatic History, 6

Edrisi, 30

Elæococca verucosa, 171

Empress Tai-Hau of the Wei dynasty, possibly the patroness of Hoei-shin, 6

Esquimaux, 11

Ethnology, accuracy in, 114
Ewbank, Thomas, 151

FA-HIAN, 89, 90 ; Travels of, 92
Fa-kiai-ngan-litu, *i.e.*, More Certain Tables of Religion, 32
Feathers, ball of, seen by Mexican goddess, 36
Fishermen, Chinese and Japanese, 66
Flying natives of Fusang, fable of, 143
Florida, Straits of, 74
Flower of the Centre, name for China, 6
Fogs in Kamtschatka, 73
Formosa, 11, 67
Foster, Y. W., LL.D., 115
Fox Islands, 11, 70.
Fruit preserved, 69
Furs in the Aleutian Islands, 132
Fusang, kingdom of, 25 *et seq.* ; latest discussions of, 142, 161 ; Fu-
    sang-tree, 45, 162 ; malvaceous, 164; envoys from Fusang to
    China, 175; not in Japan, 142, 173
Future of Eastern Asia, 46

GALLATIN Albert, 7, 56, 195
Garments and colours peculiar to the King of Fusang, 27
Gaubil, " Observations Mathématiques," 9, 40 ; researches in Chinese
    astronomy, 128
Gentleman's Magazine, 165
Geographers, early, probably possessed information relative to the North
    Pacific Ocean now lost, 147
Gipsy names for animals, 41, 164; affinities with Hindoos, 192
Gobineau, Count, his ideas as to ancient America, 176 ; regards it as the
    world's cradle, 176
Goei-chi (A.D. 510), 129
Gold in Fusang, 28
Good Hope, Cape of, 75
Great Ireland, 24
Green-corn festival of the Creek Indians, 56 ; dance of the, *ib.*
Grellon, Père, finds a Huron woman in Tartary, 137

Grijalva, Juan de, nephew of Velasquez, 36
Greek priest and family in Atcha, 69
Grotius, 127

HAKODODI, 67
Han, history of the later, 173 ; in Corea, *ib.*
Hanley, Mr, 172
Hawaiian Spectator, 44
Hei-chi, black-toothed men, 167
Herrera, Antonio de, 38
Hiao-wou-te of Souang, reign of, 155
Hibiscus rosa siniensis, called Fusang in Pekin, 170 ; *Hibiscus syriacus, ib.*
Hieronymus d'Angelis, 46
Hinds domesticated in Fusang, 154
Hiouen-thsang, life and travels of, 88
" Histoire des Huns, des Turcs, des Mongoles," &c., par Joseph Deguignes, 138
History and journeys of fifty-six monks of the dynasty of Thang, 92
History of the Master of the Law of the three collections of the Convent of Grand Benevolence, 91
Hoai-nan-tsu, the, on Fusang, 143
Hoam-ho River, 131
Hoang-hoin, 144
Hodgson, works of, 156
Hoei-shin, Hoei-schin, Hui-shên, name how written, vi. ; verification of his assertions, 187 ; narrative as translated by Professor Neumann from the Chinese, and revised by him, 3 ; meaning of the word, 25 ; his journey, 58 ; his route, 130 ; his description of the American aloe, 172 ; he confuses plants, *ib.* ; Hui-shên, " a lying priest," according to Bretschneider, 166 ; narrative of Hoei-shin as given by Bretschneider, 168
Hoei-khé Turks, 144
Hoei-li, 91
Hoei-seng and Seng-yung, memoir of, 93
Hoffmann, 14
Hong-ing-ta, the expounder of King in the times of Tang, 25

Hong Kong Island, 67
Hontan, Baron de, 137
Horne, George, 136
Horses in Fusang, 41, 51, 170
Hing-goci, native name for Kamtschatka, 15
Huitzilopotschli, 36
Humboldt, " Views of the Cordilleras," 156 ; " New Spain," 40
Hyde Clarke, 54
Hyacinth, Father, 170

ICHI, the King of Fusang, 27 ; Ichi and Irica, 52
Identity of Tartars and North American Indians, 7
Ihan, the celebrated astronomer, 15
Incas, 50 ; going forth of, 52 ; ritual of, *ib.* ; garments of, their colours,
    53 ; married their own sisters, 56
Indian women of North America greatly resemble the Chinese, 135
Iron in Fusang, 28, 172
Irving, Washington, " Knickerbocker History of New York," 127
Islands in the Aleutian Chain, Boulder, Kusha, Amtchitka, Krysi, or Rat
    Island, in the Andranof group, Tonago, Adakh, Atkha, Ammnak, 69
Itölmen, or natives of Kamtschatka, 17 ; dwellings of, *ib.* ; clothing, 19 ;
    music, 20

JAPAN, Notes and Queries on China and, 161 ; coast of, 66, 74 ; Ainos
    in, 140 ; as it was, 54 ; not Fusang, 142 ; Buddhism introduced,
    143, 156 ; *Broussonetia* in, 172 ; origin of name, 174
Japanese year-books, 12 ; annals from 661 until 696, 14 ; facetiæ, 29 ;
    junk, 44 ; Government, 45, 75 ; junk wrecked, 45 ; vessel in Ame-
    rica, *ib.* ; charts, 76 ; junk picked up, 77 ; resemblance of, to Sand-
    wich Islanders, 77 ; religion, 78 ; navigation, 81 ; early discovery of
    America by, 126 ; Wenshin N.W. of Japan, 129 ; maps, 147
Jean du Plan de Carpin, 32
Jeddo, 4
Jeso, 14 ; sea of, 130
Jesuit missionaries, 43
Jetschay, 16 ; Jetschaykno, *ib.*
Juan de Grijalva, nephew of Velasquez, 36

Juen-kien-hui-han, 14

Jipen, 174

KALOSCHEN, 10

Kampfer, the first who spoke of America as known from early times to the Japanese, 126.

Kamtschatka, 11, 14; in the time of Tang, 15; distance from Sigan, the capital of China, *ib.*; description of, by Steller, *ib.*; identity with Lieu-kuei, *ib.*; dwellings, 19; climate, *ib.*; habits of the people, *ib.*

Kang-hi, encyclopædia of, 14

Kao-thsang, the Emperor, 89

Kapilapura, King of, 5

Kara-korum, 144

Karl Gutzlaff, 45

Kennon, Colonel Barclay, his assistance, 63; letter from, 65; brief memoir of, 94; his personal knowledge of the North Pacific, 126 *et seq.*; on furs, 133

Khi-nie, itinerary of, 92

Khirgiz or Kirkis, 144

Kien-hai Lake or Baikal, 168

Kie-kia-ssu, countries of, 168

Kingdom and nobles of Fusang, 27

King-tschu, 25

Kipin, five beggar monks from, introduce Buddhism into Fusang, Kipin, and Beloochistan, 31; Kipin, Kophen, Bokhara, 155.

Klaproth, Julius von, 125; passed translation from the Chinese as his own, 12, 174; attempted to refute Deguignes, 125 *et seq.*; "Récherches sur le Pays de Fou-sang," 138; ridicules Deguignes, *ib.*; thought Tahan was Kamtschatka, 141; argument against Deguignes, *ib.*; contradicts his text according to D'Eichthal, 142, 156; according to Bretschneider, he refuted Deguignes, 166; "Tableau Historiques," 168; his disciple, Bretschneider, 176; severely judged, 183

Knonotski, Cape of, 68

Knickerbocker Magazine for 1850 contained the first English version of Neumann's work on Fusang, now given in this volume, 163

Ko-li-han, or Choran, country of, 130

Kong, the Hill of, 25

Kou-li-han, country of, 144

Kousang plant resembles the maguey, 180

Kocoima walrus-hunters often carried on ice-fields from the Asiatic to the American shore, 137

Krusenstern, Straits of, 66

Ku, country of, 168

Kuang-wu, reign of, 173

Kurile or Aleutian Islands, 11, 65, 67, 132

Kuro-suvo, or Japanese current, 71, 74

LADRONE Islands, 74

Lao-tse, 3

La Perouse, Strait of, 141

Leang, dynasty of, 24 ; Leang-schu, 25

Leao-tong, northern province of China, 128, 140

Leg of mutton, time measured by roasting, 10

Lew-Chew, Loo-Choo, natives of, without iron, 172

Li, Chinese measure of distance, 128 ; in the fifth century, 140 ; twenty thousand *li* from Tahan, 141

Liang dynasty, history of, 166

Liang-ssu-kung-ki, passage from the, stating that ambassadors went from Fusang to China, 175, 184

Liang-sze-kung-ki, the, 184

Lieu-kuei, its situation, 15 ; meaning of the word, 16 ; king of, sent his son to China, 145

Life of Gaudama, 93

Li-pe-tai on Fusang, 143

Li-sao, the, on Fusang, 143

Li-yen, a Chinese historian, speaks of Fusang, 127

Loo-chooese and Japanese, 79

Lorchas Islands, 74

MADJICO Sima group, 67

Maguey or *Agave americana*, 37, 162, 171

Malvacea, Fusang-tree, 170–180

Mamma or *ama*, found in many languages, 107

Mandans, 152 ; their heaven and hell, 153

Mandeville, Sir John, and other travellers, 33

Mantchou tribes dressed in fish-skins, 20 ; Jupi, *ib.*

Mao-jen, the hairy men, or Ainos, 12, 174

Ma (or Man) tu-an-lin, 12, 14, 24, 166

Marriage in Fusang, 46

Marvels and romances of Fusang, 32 ; marvels narrated by Hoei-shin, 94

Matsumai, 67

Maury (*vide Revue des Deux Mondes,* April 1858), 132

Mau-shin, Mosin, 11

Melendez, Pedro, 136

" Mémoirs de l'Academie des Inscriptions et Belles Lettres," 22, 125, 126, 148

Memoirs of the kingdoms of Buddha, 90

Merchants, foreign, clothed in silk among the Catacualcans, 136

Metals and money, 38

Mexican antiquities, 113 ; god of air, *ib.* ; monuments, pyramidal form of, 35 ; money, 38 ; nobility, four orders of, 39

Metals and money in Fusang, 38

Miles, Colonel, translator of the " Shajrat-ul-Atrak," his translation of " *tung,*" 9

Milk known to ancient Mexicans, 154

Mirambecs, Indians near the Great Salt Lake, 137

Mirrors brought from Fusang, 184 ; Peruvian mirrors, *ib.*

Mitla and Palenque, ruins of, 34

Moko or Mongolians, 16

Mongols, Mongol or Mog, 9

Mongolian, affinity of languages to Dakota Indian ; a Mongol resembles an Apache, 95

Montesinos, 53

Mormonism not Christianity, as stated by Dr Bretschneider, 184

Mormon country, 173

Morton, Dr S., his views of American Indians, 194

Moslem, 31

Mossman, S., on the early Japanese, 190

Mound-builders, 110 ; character of, *ib.*

Mourning for the dead in Fusang, 28

Mu-kin, 170
Mulberry-trees in Fusang, 143
Mummies in Aliaska, 192
" Münchener Gelehrte Anzeigen," 24

NAGERA, Castañeda de, 151
Naked men, lands of, 167
Names, how given by newcomers into strange lands, 164
Nan-su, the historian, 134
Narrative of Hoei-shin, with comments by Professor C. F. Neumann, 1 ;
    as given by Bretschneider, 165
Na-to-scha, nobles of Fusang, 27
Nausse or history of the southern dynasty, 22
Navigation, early Chinese, 64
Neumann, Professor C. F., memoir of, vi.; education and life, *ib.* ; his
    works, xiv.; his work on Fusang, 3 ; Neumann not read by Dr
    Bretschneider, but attacked by the latter, 178
New Spain, 36
New Mexico, early seat of ancient Mexican civilisation, 151 ; Indians of
    New Mexico, 135
Niça, Father, saw white Indians, 152
Nineveh Library, discovery of, 50
Niphon, 67
Northern California, Chinese traded with, in remote times, 136
Norsemen in America, 32
North American Indians, resemblance of, to Mongolians, 80
Notes and Queries on China and Japan, request in, for information on
    Fusang, 173 ; on Fusang, 161, 166
Nu-wang-kuo, 175

ODIN, EIGHT RINGS OF, 36
Onon, the River, 144
Orchon, left bank of, 144
Ordos or Ho-tao country, 144
Oregon, 71
" Ost-Asien und West-Amerika, Zeitschrift für Allgemeine Erdkunde,"
    April 1864, an article by Neumann which refers the nativity of
    Hoei-shin to China, 139

Ostrogoths and European nations, 8
Oxen in Fusang, 40

PACHACOMAC, 55
Pacific Islands to the leeward of Japan, 79
Papua or New Guinea, 12
Paravey, his two works on the Fusang question, 166
Parsees, the, 95
Pears in Fusang, 28
Pe-hai, North Sea, and Schao-hai, Little Sea, 16
Perez José, in *Revue Orientale et Americaine*, 142
Peru and Fusang, 49 *et seq.* ; Peruvian Incas, 50 ; houses, 51 ; cycles,
       53 ; traditions of the Deluge, 54 ; of the good Deity, *ib.* ; Peruvian
       and Chinese policy alike, 55 ; graves, 7
Peter and Paul's Haven, 15
Peti or northern savages, 9
Pictures by Chinese botanists, 179
Pi-khieou or priests of Buddha, 155
Piljo-tai-hotun, 131
Polaris, crew of, 137
Popol Vuh, 151, 154
Posten, Hon. C. D., 95
Postpositions, 107
" Prehistoric Races of the United States of America," 115
Prescott, "History of Mexico," 34, 37
Prester John, 33
Prisons in Fusang, 46, 153
Probability of voyages made by ancient Japanese, 74
Prostitution or polygamy in Utah, 182
Pueblo Indians of light colour, 135 ; cloth, *ib.* ; dwellings, *ib.*
Pun-tsao, 171
Pun-tsao-kang-mu, 170

QUIVIR, 136

RED Indians and Chinese, affinities between, 192
" Relation des Mongols ou Tartares," by Jean du Plan de Carpin, 33
Remarks on the text of Professor Neumann, 49

Renzi, " Memoires de la Société des Antiquaires, Partie linguistique," 8

" Reports of Explorations and Surveys for the Pacific Railroad," 151

Revue des Deux Mondes, 149

Revue Archæologique, 132

Roehrig, F. L. O., 100

Roger's Straits, 66

Romances of Fusang, 143 ; poets who have written on it, *ib.*

Rosny, Léon de, 169

Russian establishments on St Paul and St George, 132

SAGHALIEN, Fusang according to Bretschneider, 175 ; not in a temperate climate, 172

Sákka, Sakkū, a swan, 164

Salt Lake City, 173

Samarcand, a stronghold of Buddhism, 155 ; Bonzes from, *ib.*

San Blas, 33

Sanson, his map, 147

Sandwich Islanders resemble Japanese, 77

Saturday Review, 115

Schakia, religion of, 36

Schan-hai-king, 12

Schensi, district of, 15

Shajrat-ul-Atrak, or genealogical tree of the Turks and Tartars, 9

Shapa, capital of Loo-choo Islands, 67

Siebold, " Japanese Archives," 14

Sigan, the ancient capital of China, 15

Silver in Fusang, 28

Simson Theos., 161 *et seq.* ; approved by Dr Bretschneider, 179

Simson, William, F.R.G.S., 99

Sitka, 71, 149

Sloane, Hans, 148

Song, Great Light of, 28

Stags in Fusang, 28 ; stag-horns, 40

Stanislas, Julien, 88 *et seq.*

Steller, " Description of Kamtschatka," 14, 17

Stems, Mongol and Mantchou, 40

Sterculia plantanifolia, 171

Sultoi-Noss, 145

Sum or Sung dynasty, 145

Sun makes his toilet in Fusang, 143

Sung-yun, the mission of, 92, 93; probably contemporary with Hoei-shin, 92

TAHAN, means Great China, 24; distance, 33, 57, 127, 129; five thousand *li* between Jesso and Tahan, 131; travellers' route to, *ib.*; reached by sea, 133; Tahan to Fusang, 166; 20,000 *li*, 140; route to, 144, 146; envoys from, first came to China in seventh century, 168; according to Bretschneider in Siberia, 175

Tai-Hau, Empress Dowager, 93

Tam-chu, route to America, 131, 133

Tang dynasty, history of, 167, 174

Tang-schu or year-books of Tang, 12; ruler of Tang, 13; Kamtschatka described in the time of, 15; error in Tang-schu, 16

Tapia, Señor José Ortiz, 113

Tarai-kai, was it Tahan? 141

Tartars' Hades, 8; Tartar cycle and its colours, 53

Tattooing by Wen-shin and by North American Indians, 167

Tchitchagoff, 68

Tchung-cheou-kiang-tching, 131

Temperature of Bhering's Straits, 74; of Matsumai, 75

Ternaux Compans, 151

" The devil who runs through," *i.e.*, Lieu-kuei, 16

" The devil's companion," *i.e.*, Jetschay, 16

Thom, Mr Robert, 90

Time measured by roasting legs of mutton, 130

Tolteks, 35, 113

Tomsk, 168

Travellers, the old, not now entirely discredited because they narrated marvels, 178

Tschen, dynasty of, 11

Tschuktschi or Koljuschens, 10, 16

Tschu-tschu or Land of Dwarfs, 12

Tuilu, nobles of Fusang, 27

Tuna, Mexican word for cactus, 179

T'ung, the tree, 171

Tunguse, Turks, Mongolians, &c., identical with the Esquimaux races, 7 ; Tungese Eastern barbarians, 8 ; geographical situation of, 9 ; customs, 10

Turner, Professor W. W., 151 ; works of, 156

" UNIVERSAL Compassion," meaning of the name Hoei-shin, 25
Uries, Strait of, 130

VASCO de Gama, 75
Vasquez, Fr., de Coronado, 136
Vancouver's Island, 71
Ven-hien-tum-kao, the historian (A.D. 515), 131, 134
Vessels driven by storms to America from Asia, 134
Vestal virgins in Peru, 55 ; among the Pueblo Indians, to keep their fire burning, 195
Vine known in Mexico, 152
Viracocha, 55
Visnago, Cactœ globosœ, 179
Voyages can be made from China to America in sight of land, 71

WENJAMINOW, Father, "Sur les Isles Aleoutiennes du District de Unalaska," 149
Wen-shin or Painted People, 11, 22 ; the country of the, same as Jeso, 140
" Western Countries, Memoirs of," edited by Hioen-thsang, 91
Western Mountain of the Gods, 4
Whipple, Lieutenant A. W., report by, 151
White aborigines in Mexico, 152
Winaland or Vineland, 32
Wilson, Daniel, LL.D., " American Ethnology," 193
Wo, ancient name for Japan, 174
Women and children, Japanese and Chinese, go to sea with head of family, 77
Women, Kingdom of, in Fusang, 29 ; situated 1000 *li* east of Fusang, 134 ; tribes of aborigines in North America called women, *ib.* ; story of the Kingdom of Women only given as a report by Hoei-shin, *ib.* ; not in Japan, 142, 169 ; no *mammœ, ib.* ; suckle children, *ib.* ; kingdom, where situated, 173, 182, 286 ; in Japan, 175

Wo-nu, envoys from the, 173

Woo-sung River, 66

Wog or Mog Mongolians, 9

Wrangell, Rear-Admiral, " Les Renseignements, &c., sur les Possessions Russes," 148

Writing, Chinese, introduced into Japan A.D. 280, 174

Wu-ti, Emperor, 173

YAMATO or Ye-ma-t'ai, 175, 280

Yang-kon, Valley of, 143

Yang-tse-kiang, 66

Year-books of the Chinese Empire, 5, 15 ; of the Southern dynasty, 22 ; year-books of Leang, 22, 26

Ye-ma-t'ai, 173

Yenissey, 168

Yen-thsang, 91

Y. J. A. inquires in Chinese *Notes and Queries* as to Fusang, 161 *et seq.*

Yucatan, 73

Yu-tche, a race derived from the Che-goei, 133

Yu-t'ung tree, 171

ZENGHIS Khan or Tschinggs Chakan, 9

Zuni, white Indians at, 152

THE END.